YES, I DIRECTED "THE ROOM"

The TRUTH about directing the "Citizen Kane of Bad Movies"

by

Sandy Schklair

7190 W Sunset Blvd #86
Los Angeles, CA 90046
United States

ISBN 978-1-7751755-0-6

ISBN 978-1-7751755-4-4 (E-Book)

www.findingdimeslit.com

Acknowledgments

"I would like to gratefully acknowledge those friends of mine who allowed me to bounce ideas off their heads and help me prepare this book:
Rick Harper for his expertise and advice; Dina Khouri for her excellent photos, her emotional support and her encouragement; Geoff Mark, Rosalind Gatto and Julia Schklair for their insightful review and comments as the book slowly came together.

Thank you, my friends, for believing in me and tolerating my often misdirected passion and enthusiasm."

-Sandy

CONTENTS

Foreword.. vi

Chapter 1   For The Record 1

Chapter 2   Why Me?.. 24

Chapter 3   I Am Hired Or How I Fell Down
The Rabbit Hole 30

Chapter 4   My Approach 51

Chapter 5   The Script?.. 56

Chapter 6   The Spoons.. 73

Chapter 7   The Alley, The Rooftop And
The Psychology Office 78

Chapter 8   The Crew.. 87

Chapter 9   Tommy's Two Love Scenes Or
I Resign On The Last Day 102

Chapter 10   The Media Reacts 110

Chapter 11   The Internet 124

Everything Wrong With "The Room"
In 8 Minutes Or Less: 126

Fanboy Flicks: 129

Nostalgia Critic, The Room Review: 132

Entertainment Weekly Article – Viewer Comments:........... 135

The Morning Show: Inside The Room: 137

Chapter 12   The Final Word 139

YES,
I DIRECTED
"THE ROOM"

The TRUTH about directing the "Citizen Kane of Bad Movies"

by

Sandy Schklair

FOREWORD

In September, 2002, Tommy Wiseau produced "The Room" and hired me to direct the project for him. Tommy Wiseau was the producer, writer and lead male actor of this film. For fourteen years, he has claimed to be the Director as well. Nothing could be further from the truth. The events leading up to my writing this book may not be so funny to me personally; but, the story itself is hilarious.

The first chapter, "For The Record," is probably not as funny as the rest of the book. Sorry, but, I'm a screenwriter and like any good screenplay, I need to set the stage first. I need to "make my case" as it were. Some of you know may know a great deal about "The Room" and some of you may know nothing except what you've learned from "The Disaster Artist." I've never met James Franco or Seth Rogen, nor have I been allowed to read their script...

Director: A film Director is hired by a Producer to interpret a written script and record that script on film, tape or digital medium. The Director controls the performances of the actors and gives instructions on how he wants the dialogue interpreted and delivered during the shooting process. The Director then "blocks" the scenes with the actors. Blocking is the process of creating and directing the physical action of the actors as they deliver the scripted dialogue and act out the scripted scene. The Director then designs a series of shots that will cover the blocking of the actors. When everything has been worked out and the equipment is rolling, the Director starts the shot by saying, "Action" to initiate the actors' performances and then says, "Cut" to stop the camera. Only the Director and the Cinematographer are allowed to say "Action" and "Cut" on set.

First Assistant Director: The 1st AD runs the set for the Director and schedules the daily work. The AD gives orders to start the cameras and sound recording just prior to the Director saying "Action." The AD makes sure that all department heads (camera, sound, wardrobe, make up, hair, art, grip & electric, etc.) are ready for the next two or three shots so there is a minimum of down-time and the set runs efficiently.

Script Supervisor: The Script Supervisor is the on-set editor. This position is in charge of all continuity and makes copious notes for the post production editors regarding the individual shots and "takes," and how the film should be cut together.

In 2002, I Directed "The Room" and also performed the duties of 1st AD and Script Supervisor. I controlled the performance aspects of the actors and their delivery of the scripted dialogue. I designed the camera shots and the coverage of the scenes. I was the only person on the set to ever say "Action" or "Cut."

Within these pages, I will settle the controversy about who Directed "The Room."
I will tell you what happened on the set of "The Room." And, I will tell you why it happened. I will tell you the truth!

If you have never seen "The Room" there may be a few

references that you will not understand. I will do my best to give explanations for these references. I apologize in advance for any confusion this may create.

"The Room" has been called "The Citizen Kane of bad movies." It has been called, "The worst movie ever made." But, is it? I don't think so…

CHAPTER 1

FOR THE RECORD

I Directed "The Room" for Tommy Wiseau in 2002. I was also the 1st Assistant Director and the Script Supervisor. This is the truth, the whole truth, and nothing but the truth, so help me God.

Wow! I finally said it out loud. Here, you try saying it. I'm serious. Say it loud and proud. Wrap your mouth around these words. "Yes, I Directed the Citizen Kane of bad movies." It stings a little at first, but it gets much easier with repetition; especially when you realize that maybe it's <u>not</u> the worst movie ever made.

I'm going to do something that has never been done before in regard to the absurd little cult film known as, "The Room." I'm going to tell the truth. That's it. I'm simply going to tell the truth. Nobody has ever done that before.

Since the day this project wrapped in 2002, I have watched a small molehill of lies slowly grow into a veritable mountain range of lies – the Himalayas of lies. "The Room" is an outrageous and absurdly stupid movie… <u>which is exactly how I Directed it.</u>

YES! I Directed "The Room."

This is such a simple statement; and yet, so complex in its nature. To date, "The Room" has generated one major motion picture, one documentary, two books and countless articles in the press and online; including Entertainment Weekly, Huffington Post and The Daily Mail. My name has been bandied about in all these venues, and not always kindly. I have always preferred to take "the high road" and ignore "The Room" and the world it inhabits. Recent events have forced me to veer off the high road, put on my tire chains and start slogging through the mud. As Betty Davis once said, "Fasten your seat belts, it's going to be a bumpy night."

With the release of James Franco's "The Disaster Artist", I have been left with no choice but to make an honest public statement about my involvement in this wonderful, horrible, bizarre little movie. This book is long, long overdue -- fourteen years overdue, to be precise. During those fourteen years, I have watched with utter amazement at the insanity and -- dare I say it? -- the legend that has grown around this unbelievably absurd movie.

Second Unit for "The Room" was a San Francisco Unit that worked for a couple of weekends shooting generic exterior establishing shots and the exceptionally ridiculous Flower Shop and Coffee Shop scenes. I did not direct Second Unit.

I also did not Direct the very last day of shooting. Let's clear up a little confusion right out of the gate. "The Room" was shot here in Hollywood for one month. That's right. Ignore the rumors you've heard. I shot for one month, twelve hours per day, five days per week. I also saved Tommy's two nude love scenes for the last day of shooting... and resigned on that day. Can you blame me? I am not a religious man; yet, God heard my prayers and I was granted this small mercy. [See Chapter 9, "Tommy's Two Love Scenes (or) I Resign on the Last Day."]

I also took on the responsibilities and duties of the 1st Assistant Director and the Script Supervisor. I both laughed and worked my ass off every single day of production. Three big jobs on one tiny little feature, in one tiny little room. Tell you what... the next time you watch "The Room," be sure to pay attention to the credits. There is no 1st AD listed in the crew. What are we to think? The film set ran itself? Either this was the first movie in history to be made without a 1st AD, or someone had my name removed from the credits. Now... who would do such a thing?

My Mindset: I was Directing a movie nobody was ever going to see! Which is a shame, because I thought it was really, really funny. This is Hollywood. We make millions of horrible little movies that never see the light of day. The odds against my horrible little movie being noticed were astronomical! I knew, in the future, when I related the actual facts surrounding the "The Room," nobody would ever believe me. How could they?! Had I not been there myself, I would not have believed me either.

The statements I've made regarding "The Room" are true whether you read them in this book or hear them uttered before the Supreme Court of the United States. Truth is absolute and not open to interpretation.

True: Tommy Wiseau is the Producer of "The Room."
True: Tommy Wiseau is the Writer of "The Room."
True: Tommy Wiseau is the lead male Actor of "The Room."

NOT True: Tommy Wiseau is the Director of "The Room."

NOT True: Sandy Schklair is the Writer of "The Room."

I did not write "The Room," I did naahhht! I want to make this absolutely crystal clear. I would rather be named in a Kardashian paternity suit than be accused of writing "The Room." Director's rarely Direct scripts they've written. A Writer sells his/her script to a Producer who then hires a Director to direct the pages. Tommy Wiseau is a Producer/Writer, and he produced the glorious crumbs that tumbled out of his fevered imagination and dribbled out onto the scripted pages that were handed to me. Yes, handed to me…three pages at a time.

Producer/Writer is a very dangerous combination. There is no unbiased critic between the writing and the camera. Tommy hired me to Direct the pages. I straightened the words out every day (you have no idea…), but I did NOT write them. I am blameless. Stop pointing the judgmental fingers at me. There are simply not enough drugs or alcohol or mutational carcinogens on the planet Earth that can get words like this to roll off my fingertips. I was hired to Direct the pages that were handed to me. So, "Leave your stupid comments in your pocket." (God, I love this horrible line!)

Psychologically, if you repeat a lie often enough, you begin to believe your own fabrications. However, simply repeating the same fairy tale for fourteen years will not make it true no matter how badly you want to be a Director. Tommy Wiseau desperately wants the world to believe he is the Director of "The Room." Sorry, Tommy, whether you put your name on the slate, in the credits, or shout it out in interviews… you cannot alter the immutable fact that you did naahhht Direct this movie.

IMDB: The Internet Movie Data Base is the official

listing for all things cinematically related. When I last checked the IMDB listing for "The Room" I couldn't seem to find my name listed anywhere. That's right. My name is not even listed. What a shock, right? Director? 1st Assistant Director? Script Supervisor? Nothing. Not even Mr. Congeniality...

Do you wonder how this travesty of justice happened? Stop wondering. Tommy Produced "The Room." I won't ever dispute that. The Producer gets to decide the credits on a non-union film in Hollywood. Why hell, any non-union Producer can claim Elvis came back from the dead to direct his movie and Bugs Bunny shot it... it still doesn't make it true.

Tommy Wiseau produced "The Room." IMDB has the credits that Tommy authorized. The film itself has the credits that Tommy chose during the editing process... in the job categories he chose to list them. An unscrupulous film Producer can list any credits he wants in his project. Credits are the prerogative of the Producer. It's not fair, but... case closed.

Tommy hates me... because Tommy hates and fears the truth. Naturally, this causes me endless sleepless nights and hurts my feelings. Of course he hates me! He's been telling this fairy tale about "The Room" and about me in particular for fourteen years; and, this tale has taken on a life of its own. Tommy doesn't understand that whether I write this book or not, the truth will come out. Ultimately, eventually, without fail, the truth always comes out in Hollywood. There are countless people in Los Angeles who are paid many thousands of dollars to dig out every shred, every scrap, and every crumb of dirt that lies hidden in the dark corners of the film industry; from Rock Hudson's alien baby to Marilyn Monroe's White House trysts. The entertainment journalists and paparazzi in Los Angeles passionately live for digging out and exposing lies. Lies in Hollywood have a shelf life. Tommy's lies have a shelf life of fourteen years. They have now expired.

The fiction and half-truths that surround "The Room" have grown in scope and magnitude over the past ten years. Every time Tommy slowly begins to comprehend why people love this movie, his tales grow to encompass his new understanding. A few years ago during a televised interview, I heard him give a deep, philosophical, existential explanation for the plastic spoons gleefully thrown against the movie screen by enthusiastic fans. I couldn't believe my ears. What a pile of bullshit! The spoons were nothing more than an inside joke on the set.

I wrote Tommy many emails over the years trying to explain the nature of secrets and lies in Hollywood. He is on record endlessly saying I never contacted him after I left the project on the last day of shooting. This is simply not true. And, oh darn, I kept copies of every email I ever sent him. For example:

> *Hi Tommy,*
>
> *I think it's time we get together and discuss our unique situation. We both know that I Directed "The Room." You are NOT the Director. You have claimed to be the Director for seven years… and, as we both know, this is completely untrue.*
>
> *Tommy, I don't want to involve lawyers or newspapers in our situation. At*

least, I don't want to involve them... yet. Going into court and proving that I Directed "The Room" will be extraordinarily easy for me because <u>it is the truth!</u> Every cast and crew member involved with the production would truthfully testify that I Directed every frame of this movie. And yet, you continue to claim that you Directed this film. We need to talk about this, don't you think? (October 30, 2009, 11:01am)

Just like Nostradamus, right?

In all honesty, I don't recognize a lot of the names mentioned in the opening credits for the film. I won't mention their names here; but, the two talented gentlemen who actually worked as DP (Director of Photography) on this project – the two men who actually shot it -- aren't even credited on either IMDB or the film itself. There are three people credited on the actual film as Directors of Photography. Two of these names are a mystery to me. The third shot second unit. This is Non-Union Hollywood at its best; and, Tommy does tend to play fast and loose with the credits for this project. Producers who behave in this manner are considered dishonorable and develop horrendous reputations. Credits are the currency of Hollywood. When a project ends, our employment ends. Every film professional experiences unemployment every year of their career. A professional in Hollywood is nothing more than the sum of his/her credits.

I left on the last day of shooting for extraordinarily good reasons. I was not involved in editing and post production. Tommy, a man who has never edited a feature film in his life, oversaw the editing process for "The Room." It looks like it. And, may I just say, "Holy Shit!" The foreplay in those love scenes goes on FOREVER! And, all of it features Tommy's bare ass! I guess the editor must love foreplay too.

You shoot a lot of footage when you're creating a love scene so you can cut something beautiful out of it. You DON'T cut all the footage into the final print; unless, of course, you are in love with your own naked ass and the sound of your own fake orgasm. Eww, yuck! It is pretty funny though…

As any Director on the planet can tell you, if you're going to feature a full frame of someone's naked ass in your film a good rule of thumb is, it should be the girl's ass! . A woman's ass is much prettier and photogenic than a man's ass. If you feel the need to show a man's ass, keep it brief! Tommy's two nude love scenes are all about his ass and his orgasm noises. I'm sure we can all agree this is GROSS! Lisa is always buried beneath him. Both love scenes! His noises! His ass! (I actually gagged a little as I typed this paragraph.) The first shot in the "morning after" scene is Tommy's naked ass walking upstage. For the love of God, Man! Enough already! And, people wonder why I left on the last day of shooting…

Let's all thank God the film does NOT have any full frontal nudity. As I discovered later, that rare and wonderful treat was reserved for the sole viewing pleasure of my crew. All… Day… Long…

I've spent nearly 30 years working on feature films and television shows. Love scenes are always difficult and uncomfortable to shoot. There are rules regarding the shooting of love scenes in the non-pornographic world.

There are rules that every Director issues in order to have a comfortable set in which to shoot an uncomfortable scene. This applies equally to the cast <u>and</u> crew. I left this project on the last day of shooting because Tommy opposed my "nude love scene" rules and I refused to compromise my principals.

No matter how bizarre this movie is... no matter how absurd, how ridiculous, how incredibly idiotic, this movie is, Tommy Wiseau is simply not capable of directing this or any other movie. Good Grief, have you ever seen or heard him in an interview?! Tommy Wiseau?! Direct a movie?! On this planet?!

To date, the "worst film ever made" has spawned:

1) "The Room" - the original film;
2) "The Disaster Artist" - a book written by Greg Sestero and Tom Bissell;
3) "Room Full of Spoons" - a documentary;
4) "The Disaster Artist" - a motion picture directed by James Franco;
5) Countless articles and reviews online and in print; and
6) The book you are holding in your hands.

All this interest for "The Room?" Extraordinary! And, my involvement on these projects? Let's see...

"The Room" movie: I am only credited with being the Script Supervisor on the actual film. On the DVD, there is a feature called "Behind the Scenes." Tommy had a kid shooting videos of the entire shooting process. I was practically living on set; either shooting, problem solving or plotting the afternoon's shot list while the crew was at lunch. Tommy actually put out the effort, time and money to carefully edit me out of the entire "Behind the Scenes" piece. Sweet... Unfortunately for Tommy, it wasn't possible to cut me out of everything because I played such an integral role in making the film. You can see me in many places; and you can hear me in the background giving direction and running the set. After the project wrapped, I learned Tommy had ordered the still photographer not to take pictures of the crew or me. Thanks Tommy... what a peach.

"The Disaster Artist" book: Greg and Tom never interviewed me for their book and included only one photo of me. The book does kind of treat me fairly... more or less... sort of... You have to read between the lines to figure out what actually happened.

"Room Full of Spoons" documentary: Rick Harper, a Canadian documentary filmmaker, flew to Los Angeles with a small crew and interviewed me in my home.

Rick is a terrific guy and he's going to tell the truth. I believe him. His film will annoy an awful lot of people who have been telling an awful lot of lies. I must also point out that I'm now 80lbs lighter than I was when Rick interviewed me. Don't judge...

"The Disaster Artist," motion picture: This movie was being shot as I wrote these words. In all honesty, I'm a huge fan of Seth Rogen and James Franco. like their movies. They seem like honorable, upright men. I sent an email to Seth who then passed my name to his Screenwriter... who never wanted to meet me or talk to me. I sent a few more emails to Seth during the ensuing months. They all went unanswered. I left phone messages with his Agent and Manager. They went unreturned. I left messages with his Production Company. They went unreturned. I left messages with the "The Disaster Artist" production office. "Hi, this is Sandy Schklair. You know, the guy Seth is portraying in your film... which is going to be released all over the planet Earth. Would you please have your Producers call me." Dead silence. I swear I heard crickets and tumbleweeds blowing around in the background. I like Seth Rogen. I respect both he and James Franco. Naturally, I'm bewildered that he doesn't even want to meet and talk to the man he is portraying in his film. It really is surprising that nobody on this project wants to talk to me.

The guys at Entertainment Weekly told me this was because nobody wants to know that Santa Claus doesn't exist. Santa Claus... Tommy Wiseau...Okay, I get it. Fine.

You want to tell the story the way you want to tell the story; although, it would have been nice if someone, somewhere, wanted to actually speak to the Director of the original film. Seth Rogen is playing me, after all. Imagine this was you. Imagine fate placed you in my shoes... Imagine you are a character written into a script... written by someone who has never spoken to you. A little unsettling, right? Perhaps a wee bit pissifying? He's speaking for me... with words that aren't mine... to the entire world. I can only pray I am treated fairly. Any lies or half-truths in the Franco/Rogen film could actually hurt my career and the distributor is planning a world-wide release. Oh, joy... I guess I'll have to wait for the film to come out to discover whether or not I still have a film career.

Note: The day after I gave a five minute phone interview to The Daily Mail and used the word "snubbed." The producers of "The Disaster Artist" called me. They repeatedly said they wanted "to open lines of communication so I wouldn't feel snubbed." I guess they read the article. They were gracious, courteous, and respectful. We had a lovely little superficial chat about nothing at all, and communicated with an understanding veteran filmmakers tend to achieve after surviving a few decades in Hollywood. They just kept repeating the "communication/snubbed" line as an answer to every comment I made. I appreciated their perspective. I was assured Seth would not play me as an imbecile. Oh, goodie... imagine my relief.

Of course, nobody wants to talk to me about the Sandy Schklair character. I get it... I'm not part of their project...

What the fuck do I know about Sandy Schklair?

This Book: Finally! Somebody is willing to speak honestly about "The Room." Yeah... me. Such is life.

[When I handed my credit card to the kid running the register in Sears today, he recognized my name and asked for an autograph and a selfie... "Why yes, I did direct the Citizen Kane of bad movies." Oh, Crap...]

I hate to burst the collective bubbles of the fans of Tommy the Director; but, Santa Claus does not really exist. Neither does the Easter Bunny, the Tooth Fairy or Tommy Wiseau the Director. I'm sorry to be the one to shatter childish delusions, no matter how wonderfully bizarre they may seem. Tommy the Director does <u>not</u> exist.

Tommy the Actor exists, sort of... I Directed his acting and told him what to do in minute detail... over... and over... and over... and over... and over... Tommy has a very short attention span... and English is NOT his native language.

Tommy the Writer exists... in the sense that he does indeed have fingers... and these fingers did indeed tippy-tap on some sort of word processing keyboard.

I cleaned up the dialogue for my actors every day, and tried to give it the structure the English language deserves. I did my best to preserve the basic dialogue, such as it was. Tommy's dialogue is unique to say the least. He fought with me endlessly about this. "Sandy, don't touch, is GENIUS!"

Tommy the Producer definitely exists. I'll never take this away from Tommy. Without Tommy's producing and marketing efforts, "The Room" would never have been made, nor would it ever have been seen. Yes. Tommy did that; but, Tommy the Director? This person does not exist. This never happened. I am always amazed that people think he Directed this movie. Some people think the Earth is flat. Some people find it difficult to chew gum and walk at the same time.

There is one thing you must understand completely before reading further. Tommy IS Johnny. They are one and the same man. What you see on screen is Tommy. He is not acting. Aha! Insight! Tommy... Johnny... The names even rhyme! Tommy/Johnny, on screen or off, is the same person. Just because the camera stopped rolling doesn't mean the melodrama of the mad tea party came to an end. Dealing with Tommy/Johnny off camera was almost as much fun as dealing with Tommy/Johnny on camera. Hint: The first thing you have to do is get him to focus on your eyeballs. Unless you make this happen, you're fucked. Just like the rooftop scene...

I read a completely deranged quote of Tommy's in a magazine interview. When the reporter asked Tommy about Sandy Schklair, he said, "He was hired as a script supervisor," he says. ""Just because Sandy said Action and Cut, designed the shots, and told the actors what to do in the scenes, doesn't make him the Director! REALLY?! Out of the mouth of babes...

Calling me his assistant is insulting to the extreme. I am no man's assistant! I simply lack the temperament for being an assistant. This obstinate attitude of mine is probably left over from Medical School... which is another story entirely.

Question: If the man was busy producing, writing, acting, and learning how to chew gum and walk at the same time, exactly WHEN did he have time to direct?

Answer: Tommy Wiseau was NEVER on set unless he was acting. Period.

I have read countless comments about me on the internet over the years. Comments floating around on countless websites... all written by writers and fans who have never bothered to actually talk to me. My motives have always been questioned. "Schklair wants more money!" "Schklair wants to steal the project!" "Schklair wants to usurp Tommy Wiseau!" Usurp? Big word for a tiny mind.

Enough!! To date, I have never asked for one penny from anybody. Ever! I was hired to do a job. I am a veteran film professional.

There are a lot of guys like me floating around Hollywood. I was paid a daily rate to direct this movie for Tommy Wiseau, my Producer. This is the truth. I am an honorable man. I have never asked Tommy for more money.

Now... all bitching and moaning aside... You have to admit, by any reasonable standard of measurement, "The Room" is hilariously funny, extremely stupid and hypnotically engaging; sort of like driving by a fatal auto accident. You simply have to look. This is due to many factors: my creative efforts as the Director combined with Tommy's crazy dialogue and his unique on screen persona. I took the materials I was given and made the movie I wanted to make. I made an absurd, bizarre, weird little melodrama. This was my intent. THIS WAS ON PURPOSE!

I have been asked repeatedly, why would I want credit for directing the worst movie ever made? Why would I want to be the man known for directing the "Citizen Kane of Bad Movies?" Oh Hell, why wouldn't I? I had fun. Fun! That's why. Not everything in life is about money! This is why Raphael Smadja (the Director of Photography) called me and pressured me to meet Tommy Wiseau, and become attached to the project. Raphael and I share many similar points of view. We are friends; and, we had a bucket load of fun making this movie!

What? You think I made "The Room" for the money; or that I took the project seriously?! Oh, please!

Anybody even remotely connected to the film industry will have no problem understanding my comments. Why on Earth would anybody believe I actually took this project seriously? I never took this project seriously! I would have to be certifiably insane to approach this project as a serious filmmaker. In spite of what my friends might tell you, I assure you I am completely sane. I Directed this film exactly the way I intended to direct this film – absurd, mindless, hilarious, bizarre and incredibly stupid. To date, "The Room" has millions of fans the world over. How about that?

A huge percentage of the projects most feature film crew's work on are terrible scripts and terrible stories. These scripts are usually funded by rich relatives, rich parents or rich deluded wackos. Please, try and figure out which category this project fits in. I dare you. I Directed "The Room" as homage to every horrible little feature film I ever worked on during the course of my career in Hollywood. Even brilliant Directors like Steven Spielberg and Ridley Scott had to work on films like this during their careers. If you do it right, you have a chance to make something noticeable.

My friends, I Directed every scene so far over the top the actors needed oxygen simply to survive the dialogue. I was not trying to make a great film! I was trying to make a funny film. I took a crate of lemons the size of the Grand Canyon and created an ocean of absurdly funny lemonade.

I never laughed so much in my life. If you think this is funny on screen, you should have seen this insanity in person! I can't even begin to tell you how many times I had to cut camera and go for another take simply because my camera operator was laughing so hard he couldn't keep the camera steady. Tommy never understood this... Tommy never even saw it... and, this is what made it work! This is what made it noticeable!

I had fun! That's it. There's nothing deeper going on here. My cast and crew were having fun. With the exception of a few key personnel, everybody was working on their first or second project. So what? Who cares? We all have to start somewhere. All veterans were green at the beginning of their careers. Most of us remember that. "The Room" was a great learning experience for the beginners. I believe it is the duty and obligation of all film veterans to pass the craft on to those that follow in our footsteps. I'm not alone with this belief. Nobody learns how to be a film professional in school.

Several years ago I was sitting on set with Malcolm McDowell, bitching and moaning about another magazine article featuring "The Room" wherein Tommy was pontificating about his brilliant and insightful Directorial abilities. I went off. Malcolm and I have been friends for nearly 20 years; and, he was a very handy target for my rant. Shortly thereafter, I was contacted by the editors of Entertainment Weekly.

Me: Hello?
EW: Is this Sandy Schklair?
Me: Who wants to know?
EW: This is Entertainment Weekly.
Me: Get the fuck out…
EW: We got a call today from Malcolm McDowell.
Me: Do tell? (uh–oh, this can't be good)
EW: He said you're the guy who really Directed "The Room." Is this true?
Me: Yeeess… (20 people shriek with laughter – speaker phone – awesome)
EW: We knew it! We knew it! (yelling into the speaker)
Me: Knew what?!
EW: We knew that (bleep bleep) couldn't have Directed "The Room!"
          We always knew there was a guy like you behind this stupid movie!

> We've been looking for you for eight years!

Me: Lucky me…

The following day I was interviewed by Clark Collis of Entertainment Weekly. (February, 2011)

Fine. Great. And yet, the gist of the article was that a controversy existed as to who actually Directed the film. Really? A controversy?! Sorry, there is no controversy!

No matter their level of experience, my crew and my actors saw precisely what I was doing. Everybody got IT!

Nobody, and I mean NOBODY, took this project seriously! Well… that's not strictly true. There was one person on that project who maintained a brooding and compellingly mysterious demeanor. Yes, Marlon Brando… no, wait, that can't be right… It would appear that while I was making a bizarre, stupid, funny, over the top little comedy, Tommy Wiseau was making "Streetcar Named Desire." For me, this was irresistible! Can you imagine?! A mountain of film equipment, a crew, a small sound stage, and my very own Marlon Brando! Holy Mother of God it just doesn't get any better than this!

Regardless of the ludicrous situations I put my actors into, Tommy was always intense and convinced he was on the way toward his first Oscar win. I had my very own Stanley Kowalski. Tennessee Williams and Elia Kazan would have been insanely jealous. I actually got to direct juicy little tidbits like, "You are tearing me apart, Lisa!" By the way, that was not Take 1. Take 1 was delivered quietly, woodenly and into his shirt. It was only when I told Tommy I needed the pedestrians on La Brea Boulevard to hear him deliver the line that I got the version I wanted. That's pretty much true for the entire film. This is not a two or three Take movie. Hell, it took me more than twenty takes on the rooftop to get Tommy to actually look up and see Mark before he delivered his epic "Oh, Hi Mark." Dude, you need to look up and actually see him before you say "Hi" to him. He never quite understood that.

Speaking of multiple takes... I don't want to hear any more snarky criticism about the out-of-focus spots in "The Room." In order for the 1st Assistant Cameraman to pull focus on my inexperienced actors, the actors needed to precisely hit their focus marks. This was not ever going to happen with any degree of dependability. Do you have any idea how many things can go wrong during a single take on "The Room"?! Focus marks were the least of my worries. I was up to my eyeballs in problem solving! This is not Stage #1 at Universal! This is much, much trickier... Given my battleground, I was not going to go for another take every time the actors or the 1st AC blew a focus mark. Neither would you. Neither does Clint Eastwood.

I was working in Bulgaria on "Thick as Thieves" (Morgan Freeman, Antonio Banderas) when the popularity of "The Room" began to skyrocket upwards. I had no idea this was happening. I had been shooting in Eastern Europe for four months. I was out of touch. I finally stepped off my plane in Los Angeles; and, to my utter horror and amazement, "The Room" was being advertised EVERYWHERE! Oh My God! This can't be happening! I was stunned! How?! How?! How?!

A close friend (in the industry) met me at the baggage carousel wearing a Hawaiian shirt and a shit-eating grin. "Dude, throw your bags in the trunk. We're going to The Egyptian. There's a line around the block to see your movie." Say what?!!!

An hour later, I walked up to the box office at the theater and tested the waters. "Um… I'm the guy who really Directed this movie." They freaked out! You would have thought Martin Scorsese was standing in front of their window begging to be allowed inside -- surreal to say the least!

I stood behind the back row and observed. Men and women in the audience were dressed like my characters… they spoke the dialogue in unison with Tommy and Greg… they threw plastic spoons at the screen… Plastic spoons! At the screen! Holy Shit! My chin hit the floor and I fled for the car! My life's path had come to a rather bizarre fork and it seems I had taken the road less traveled. This, of course, is a huge understatement. Robert Frost never would have survived.

Please. Ask me again why I would want to direct this movie. Sure, "The Room" is a lot of fun in a movie theater. However, live and from four feet away? I almost peed myself laughing every day. You cannot pay for entertainment like this! Living in an asylum for the creatively deranged is very, very bad. Visiting an asylum for the creatively deranged and shooting a movie there is a ton of fun!

I Directed the dialogue and characters in the only way possible given the Producer/Actor/Writer I was working with. I made a plan and stuck with it. Just imagine what would have happened if this movie had been made without a plan?!

Regardless of the content, this movie would have been un-cut-able in editing and unwatchable to the viewer (best straight line in this book). I kept things simple and consistent. I left the ridiculous continuity errors in place, and even added more. It was funny! Don't forget, I primarily work in Hollywood as a script supervisor. I have been in charge of continuity for a great number of feature films and television shows. Continuity errors do not slip by me unnoticed. They slip by me noticed and on "The Room" they were even encouraged. The sheer mountain of discontinuity was good for my soul. I put a great deal of the "Funny" in this movie and I'm quite proud that it got noticed. Wouldn't you be? And, no, I didn't do it alone. Nobody makes a movie by themselves.

"The Citizen Kane of Bad Movies!" How cool is that?!

I met Malcolm McDowell nearly 20 years ago while working on a fun little horror film called "The Gardner", which also starred Angie Everhart. We've been friends ever since. His anecdotes regarding Kubrick and "Clockwork Orange" and priceless to me. Recently, we worked together for 3 seasons on the TNT television show "Franklin & Bash". He's a terrific friend, and I cherish the time we spend together

On the set with Antonio Banderas and Morgan Freeman while working on the 2009 thriller "Thick as Thieves". Both men are consummate professionals and a joy to work with. I spent a lot of time with Morgan between lighting setups signing old songs my father taught me from the 1940's and 1950's. Antonio always mugged for my camera when I took continuity stills. He has never lost his love for film making

CHAPTER 2

WHY ME?

The Big Question: How did I end up in that place at that time? That's fair. First, you need a little background on what, exactly, I do for a living.

I've written and sold scripts in Hollywood. The vast majority never get made. This is normal for a screenwriter. I've never quite had the courage to devote myself to screenwriting full time. To me, this seems like an excellent way to end up living in a cardboard box beneath the 405 Freeway.

I've Directed second unit days on many of the films I've worked on. This includes car chases, fights, wide establishing shots and countless other shots that support the first unit Director. This frequently includes directing insert shots, where you shoot the details, i.e., the phone, the book, the glass breaking, the speedometer, etc.

I have, however, spent the majority of my career working as a script supervisor. An experienced script supervisor is the on-set editor. It's a tough job and I really enjoy the challenge. When the cameras are rolling, a script supervisor is responsible for all continuity, keeps track of the timing of all takes, supervises the accuracy of the dialogue, consults on the editorial aspect of shots and prepares myriad notes for the editorial staff to cut the film with in Post Production. Basically, a script supervisor represents Post Production on set. A script supervisor is often referred to as "the silent Director."

A Script Supervisor needs to be wire tight and completely focused at all times. When a 'Scripty' screws up, you don't find out until two or three days later. This tends to piss off <u>everyone</u>. You are politely notified of your egregious error by the gentle and understanding words, "You are so fucking fired!" I've never been fired, not once in my entire career. This is a point of pride with me. (Frankly, that beer bottle was NOT my fault...)

Speaking of continuity... I've gotten a lot of grief over the years regarding the preponderance of continuity errors in "The Room." Take a breath and think about it for a moment. Would you prefer this film with or without continuity errors? Exactly! Stop yelling at me! I intentionally let the discontinuity slide. Those errors completely add to the wonderful chaos and humor I was creating on set. You know what was <u>really</u> funny? Raphael was the only other person on set who even noticed the discontinuity. For some reason, this really killed him. He laughed his ass off constantly! That's why I had to stick his butt outside.

My favorite discontinuity wasn't even my fault or intent. The background cityscapes on the rooftop scenes constantly change, regardless of the perspective of the camera. Perfect!
That rooftop was as surreal as the rest of the film. See? It matched! Man, that's good discontinuity!

A script supervisor sits in the hot seat. I am always within arm's reach of my Director. Close enough to tap the

Director on the shoulder and let him/her know that things have gone awry. A nice way to say, stop wasting time and film, and cut your shot. We've got to go again. I would say one of the most valuable skills for a script supervisor to develop is <u>tact</u>. If you're going to bust an "A List" Director or actor for screwing things up, you better learn to do it quietly or you're not going to survive long enough to even have a career in the first place. Every Director needs to be handled differently, depending on <u>their level of experience</u> and their personality quirks. All artistic types have quirky personalities… including me.

Anecdote: The great Zalmon King – a <u>very</u> talented "love scene" Director – was extremely high strung when the cameras are rolling. I worked on a seven month project with Zalmon that started in Spain and worked its way through Germany and Luxembourg ("Chromium Blue"). When I was hired, I knew that Zalmon would be screaming at me every day, all day, for the next seven months because I was the nearest warm body with thick skin. I added hazard pay to my deal memo. Zalmon happily paid me an extra $100 per day for the privilege of screaming at me for no apparent reason. Spittle would fly out of his mouth and hit my glasses. For an extra $2,000 per month (and the cost of the Wet-Wipes I bought to clean my glasses – I billed him),
I took it all with a smile. I only threatened him with bodily injury twice in seven months. Not bad, if I do say so myself.

I was standing next to Zalmon, shooting outside an ancient castle in Luxembourg, when he got a phone call from Stanley Kubrick. You could actually hear the eyeballs of every guy on the crew swivel in Zalmon's direction. C'mon, it was Saint Kubrick. He's a film God! "Well, Stanley, why don't you put everyone in masks. The women should be nude and the men should be in tuxedos." Oh no... ("Eyes Wide Shut")

You can learn a lot from really experienced, "A List" Directors. Making shot suggestions to one of these guys is borderline suicidal. I am not suicidal. I was sitting next to Jonathan Demme on a small project early in my career. The man is a walking graduate film professor. Jonathan saw me lean in for a comment and then watched as I changed my mind. He told me, "Never stop making those quiet suggestions to me. I may reject 95% of them... but, if you keep muzzling yourself, I'm not going to hear the 5% that I really need to listen to. Don't take it personally and, for God's sake, don't embarrass me." This means you don't yell at him across the set and tell him he fucked up his last shot. You quietly take him aside and tell him the last shot is not quite working... Sir.

Most of the Directors you work with in your career are not Jonathan Demme, or anybody else with one or two Oscars on their shelves. Every script supervisor in Hollywood spends a significant portion of their career nursing first and second time Directors through their projects. Lions Gate and Miramax used to hire me specifically for this purpose. This can be a lot of fun too. You take a much more active part in designing shots and scenes. You get to teach; and I really enjoy teaching. However, directing an actor's performance is ALWAYS the job of the Director credited with the project. This is basic. This is the LAW. I won't discuss performance with an actor unless I am directing that actor's performance. I respect the etiquette of film making and that's a line I will not cross. If I am controlling and shaping an actor's performance or the actor's interpretation of a character, then I am directing the movie. Period. This is not open to debate. I controlled and shaped all actor performances on

"The Room."

Tommy is an actor (sort of)… and he has the role of 'Director' down pat. All you have to do is hang a pair of headphones around your neck and carry an empty notebook in your hand. He also knows how to order the camera crew to keep his name on a piece of yellow tape on the slate. However, pretending to be a Director and actually being a Director are two entirely different things. He discovered this unpleasant truth when he purchased a million dollars' worth of film equipment and had no fucking idea what to do with it. Pretending to be a Director will only get you to the sound stage door. Once you go through that door, you actually require skills and experience, no matter how stupid, inane and ridiculous your vision turns out to be. When that bit of truth smacked Tommy in his pasty white nose he was forced to hire me to actually do the work. I started shooting "The Room" within one hour of being hired. That's right, no prep… I actually started directing a feature film at that very moment I was hired; and, without ever having seen a script! Can you imagine?

Think about this for a moment, please. Roll this around in your head for a while. Do you think Tommy would have let someone like me anywhere near that stage if he could have avoided it? Not a chance!
Tommy Wiseau never designed a single shot. He never Directed performance. He never staged a single scene. Not ever! Tommy Wiseau was never on set as anything other than an actor. He did manage to pose next to the camera for publicity stills. Although, to be quite honest, I really don't think he knew which end of the camera to look into.

"Sandy! Where do I look through?!" Tommy loved posing for publicity stills next to the camera with his hand on the focus knob. Sadly...he never knew it was the focus knob.

"My name is on the slate. This means, I am Director!" No, its doesn't. It means you're an egotistical producer who ordered the camera crew to put your name on the slate and remove the cinematographer's name. A piece of tape does not make you a Director.

CHAPTER 3

I AM HIRED
or
HOW I FELL DOWN THE RABBIT HOLE

The life of a film professional in Los Angeles is, without question, a bizarre and fairly surreal existence. Those of us who survive do so because we embrace the bizarre and surreal aspects of the film business; and, it becomes normal for us. You either accept the arena for what it is when you arrive or you won't survive. It's just that simple. One of my favorite aspects of the film industry is the people who work in it. They're all strong Type A personalities -- no followers, only leaders. These people work 16 hours per day and persevere with grit and determination. I have a degree in Clinical Psychology, bizarre and surreal works for me on so many, many levels.

"The Room" is not the most bizarre and surreal film of my career! Not by a long shot...

I was working on "War, Inc.," (John Cusack, Marissa Tomei, Ben Kingsley, Hillary Duff and Dan Akroyd). This is a pretty good movie. If haven't seen it, you should. We were shooting in Bulgaria and using a 150 year old, unoccupied, rundown, filthy Turkish bathhouse as an Insane Asylum. The only lighting was smoking torches on the walls and yellow emergency lights.

We had 300 nearly insane background players (some actually bussed over from a nearby asylum) dressed in the most *disgusting* outfits. A wrestling match was being staged in the main pool (no water) and the screaming Master of Ceremonies was being played by Ben Cross... in foot long dreads. The wrestlers were the prophets of the four major religions. At the end of the match, a missile comes through the roof and blows the wall down. The inmates go streaming outside and are mowed down by a line of tanks. John and Marissa were taking refuge in the Asylum before the missile hit. After our first complete Master Shot (wide shot, entire scene, multiple cameras), John came running over to me in a fit of actor passion, "Sandy, how was it?! That was fucking amazing?! That was fucking crazy! Come on! Let's do it again!" Sure, why the Hell not? Maybe we can do better... That was easily the weirdest scene I've ever worked on; and, of course, it never got cut into the movie... That scene was so over the top it was in orbit. Then, toward the end of the movie, Ben Kingsley gets hit with a cruise missile!

The actor hired to play the Submarine Commander was carousing in a brothel the night before his two scenes were scheduled to be shot; and, he got arrested when the place got raided. I was drafted for the role because I fit his costume. I even had two lines of dialogue... I went with my parents to the Los Angeles screening and I never told them I was in the movie. When I popped up on screen and fired my missile, my mother screamed. Awesome!

Rewriting a complicated scene with John Cusack and Marissa Tomei on the set of "War Inc." while shooting in Bulgaria.

Ben Cross, our "screaming" Master of Ceremonies

I've been a film professional for nearly 30 years. This stuff happens all the time. This stuff is normal for me. I worked for three months on a film about a fictitious war. We shot a dancing chorus line of gorgeous amputees singing the praises of the latest missile defense system; and, the Vice President (Dan Akroyd) issued his orders to John Cusack while sitting on the toilet of his airplane. I saw nothing odd about dressing up as a Submarine Commander and shooting a cruise missile at Ben Kingsley.

Directing "The Room" was not really all that bizarre and surreal for me.

I love the film business. You dress as odd as you choose, groom yourself as weird as you want; and, really let your freak flag fly. The only thing that truly matters is how good you are at your job. That's it. Nothing more. How good are you at your job?! One of the best gaffers (master of all things electrical) I ever worked with always wore jogging shorts (rain, snow, hurricanes, wrath of God, whatever), long sleeve T's and a 4" Mohawk with red tips on his spikes. He was also highly educated and most assuredly marched to the tune of his own personal drummer.

Our work days are never less than 12 hours, and frequently tend to be 13 or 14 hours when you add in wrap; and, that one last excruciating shot the Director has deemed 'critical to the artistic integrity of the piece.' "We just gotta have it, Man!" We travel like gypsies to distant locations, and we work with extremely quirky Type "A" personalities. Frankly, if you don't have an aggressive Type "A" personality and an emotional skin as thick as rhino hide, you will never survive. I once saw a producer start crying on set... I didn't quite know how to react until a crusty 250lb Grip yelled out from behind the lights, "Hey! Asshole! There's no fucking crying in film!" Yeah, that seemed about right. You surround yourself with a Kevlar coated happy space, plaster a smile on your face and keep the bitching and moaning to a bare minimum. Nobody wants to be around a pain in the ass; and certainly not for 12-14 hours. I worked on a series of commercials for Mattel and our last day was 22 hours. That day paid my rent...

You hear things non-film professionals would never hear

or ever understand. And yet, it all seems so completely normal to me as I type these words...

On "Devil's Rejects" (Rob Zombie) I heard the words, "We're going to need another barrel of blood on set tomorrow. You know, for when we tear his face off and hit him with a truck." Wow, that shit comes in barrels? Who knew?

On "After the Storm" (Armand Assante, Benjamin Bratt, Jennifer Beals, Stephen Lang) we were shooting in a filthy jungle in central Belize when I heard, "Dude, don't put your gear there. That's quicksand." He wasn't kidding. I also picked up a parasite in my pancreas that almost killed me twice, and left me with a light tremor in my hands from residual nerve damage.

This business is <u>not</u> for the faint of heart. This business takes courage! I've had many careers in my life. This is the hardest, and most rewarding, career I've ever had.

Mugging for the camera with Sid Haig and Bill Moseley on the set of "The Devils Rejects"

Sid Haig is a gentleman, a scholar and a friend. Making a film with Sid involves hard work and an abundance of laughs.

You live your life completely without financial security. You never quite know where your next job is going to come from; nor do you ever know what that next job may entail. I like that aspect. It's like a grab bag that your life is depending on. Maybe I'll get nothing and move into the YMCA. Maybe I'll get "Saving Private Ryan" and my career will skyrocket for a while. Maybe it'll be a feature... or a TV series... or a commercial... or background plates for a new video game coming onto the market. All features wrap. All TV shows come to an end. All projects expire. And then, you start hunting for your next gig. Unemployment is a way of life for us. Film credits are the currency of our careers. You do not screw around with credits...

In the Fall of 2002, I had just finished a large, lengthy project. I was exhausted and needed down time. This means, I was unemployed, between gigs and available for work. Making "The Room" was more fun than a month in Vegas – a bit of rest and relaxation with my good friends, Surreal and Bizarre. directing "The Room" was/is infinitely more fun and entertaining than watching "The Room." Can you imagine what that set was like?! I nearly died laughing every day. I stopped laughing five years later…

Tommy Wiseau and Greg Sestero had a relationship long before "The Room" was made. That relationship is being portrayed in, "The Disaster Artist," by the Franco brothers. I entered the history of this project on the day "The Room" began shooting.
That very day! I can only write about what happened after that day.

Tommy Wiseau rolled into Hollywood (from the East…) and was determined to make his epic film. He was also convinced he was going to win an Oscar and become famous as a film God… like Kubrick. Some of this he actually succeeded in accomplishing. Kudos to Tommy! I mean it. Writing and producing your own movie is not easy. Hollywood is filled with starving producers. Perhaps Tommy's fame didn't happen the way he envisioned, but fame is fame, right? Maybe not…

In 2002, Tommy walked into Birns & Sawyer, one of Hollywood's largest equipment rental houses and did the unthinkable! He bought over $1 Million Dollars' worth of film equipment. This is sheer insanity. Nobody does this. Nobody! No film professional in their right mind would do this. This is nuts! Only a newbie without experience and more money than sense would do this. Any equipment you buy on Monday is going to be obsolete by Wednesday. Christmas came early for Birns & Sawyer and Tommy was Santa Claus. I wasn't there; but, I'm sure there was a lot of frantic eye contact, knocking on wood, prayers muttered to a wide variety of deities; and plenty of fast talking, "Sir, if you buy that camera, you simply must buy a set of prime lenses... and, don't forget the filters." "Sid, call my wife, the kids are going to college!"

Enter Raphael Smadja. Raphael is an elderly gentleman with a lifetime of experience in Hollywood. Like any professional cinematographer in Los Angeles, Raphael had an account at B&S and owed them some bucks and, perhaps, a favor or two. This is normal. Naturally, Birns &Sawyer included Raphael with the equipment package Tommy foolishly purchased. This is not normal. I'm sure you can see where this is heading. As long as Raphael kept Tommy happily prepping and shooting... and not returning the equipment he bought within the first 30 days, Birns &Sawyer would consider all money and favors paid back. Ahh... Hollywood at its finest!

Only Tommy Wiseau, an inexperienced Hollywood newcomer, would buy two cameras in two different formats – an Arri BL film camera and a Panasonic HD tape camera.

Film professionals <u>rent</u> cameras! If there was more room on the dolly, Tommy would have taped on a cell phone, a tape recorder and a maybe a toaster oven...

I came along 13 days after the equipment had been purchased. Raphael promised me he would shoot the first 17 days of the project. Period. Not negotiable. Not going to happen! When day 17 ended, the speed of Raphael's departure could be measured in milliseconds. He sprinted to his car, threw a "Goodbye Sandy" out the window and sped off into the sunset. Yeah... good-bye Raphael... Hello, Graham! (Graham would like to keep a low profile...)

As I said, just prior to being hired to direct "The Room," I had wrapped a large, meaningful and satisfying project. It was good work. I was proud of my efforts. I was also exhausted and ready for decompression and recovery. It was a tough project that consisted primarily of 14-16 hour days and I was seriously sleep deprived.

So, there I was... floating in my tiny pool... enjoying a bit of Clapton... altering my state of consciousness with margaritas and such... The phone rings. I ignore it. The phone rings again. I ignore it. The phone rings a third time and I answer. It's a frantic phone call from Raphael. He begged, he pleaded, he whined, he cajoled (I love that word) that I meet him <u>immediately</u> in the prep room of Birns & Sawyer in Hollywood. I tried to bail out. I was tired. I was altering my consciousness. For God's sake, Clapton was playing. I had earned my down time, dammit! Raphael was insistent, "I know you're fucking around in your pool! Get out of your pool, throw on one of your stupid Hawaiian shirts; and get your ass down to Birns & Sawyer right now! I swear; you won't regret this! Trust me!" He fought dirty. He used the words "Trust me." Sigh... One hour later, I walked into the Birns & Sawyer prep room wearing a damp Hawaiian shirt. I love Raphael. There are not a lot of guys who can get me out of my pool when I'm tired and altering my state of consciousness.

Equipment rental houses in Hollywood are all designed around a similar theme. You walk through the front door into a large showroom featuring a vast array of shiny film equipment. Millions of dollars' worth of equipment... an endless sea of buttons to push, dials to twist, lenses to look through... Basically, a film nerd's wet dream. It's irresistible! I belong here. This is my church. These are my people.

When you get past the showroom – and you better have a damn good reason to get past the showroom – you enter the equipment prep room. These come in all shapes and sizes. The one over at Panavision is half the size of a football field. (I drooled on my keyboard when I typed that.)

The Prep Room at Birns & Sawyer is smaller than Panavision's. There are counters with sales staff behind them and stalls along one of the walls, much like the stalls in a barn. There are usually focus charts and color charts fixed to the stall wall.

When a DP is prepping for a project, he/she and the camera assistants use their stall for gathering the equipment that will be loaded on the camera truck and used for the entire run of the feature or show. You really don't want to run back and forth to a rental house every time you need a specific piece of equipment. Should that happen, you are informed of your error with the words, "You are so fucking fired!" This is a popular phrase in the film industry and used often and with great relish, usually by UPM's and Line Producers.

When I walked into Birns & Sawyer on that unremarkable morning in September of 2002, I was 46 years old and had been a fairly successful Script Supervisor for nearly 15 years. Successful in this case means I was able to survive doing what I love in a business that tends to destroy dreams and crush souls.

There were 3 crews in the Prep Room gearing up for projects and 2 guys behind the counter. The stalls were filled with cameras, cases, carts and tripods. I knew most of the people there because: 1) The film industry in Los Angeles really is a relatively small community; 2) I had worked with most of these people before; and, 3) I've been doing this for a long time. I was greeted in typical film fashion -- plenty of hugs, pats on the back and a rousing chorus of, "What the fuck are you doing here?" The answer to that question was standing at the far end of the Prep Room and grinning from ear-to-ear. Raphael!

We hugged, we patted and I asked him why I was standing in the B&S Prep Room wearing a Hawaiian shirt and flip flops. Raphael grabbed my shoulders, told me I was "desperately needed" and would I pleeeeeze wait and meet Tommy Wiseau – the Producer of his project – who was not there, but due at any moment. I didn't really need the work, but Raphael was positively exuberant and his intensity was definitely piquing my interest. In retrospect, I completely understand his emotional state. Raphael knows me fairly well. He figured once I met Tommy Wiseau I would feel an insatiable need to capture him on film and share him with the universe. Raphael was correct...

I waited nearly an hour for Tommy's arrival. I chatted with my friends; I played with the shiny toys, and I was just beginning to write up an invoice for my wasted time... when in walked Tommy Wiseau. This was the first time I ever laid eyes on the man -- pearly white skin, shuffling gait, sleeveless black t-shirt, and a white hat pulled down past the bridge of his nose... An eerie silence descended over the bustling room. Camera assistants and counter men were frozen in place. These people are professionals. They have experience with surreal and bizarre. Nobody moved. It was as if Medusa herself had walked in and gazed upon the room. You could have heard a pin drop! It seems I was going to have a live audience for my job interview...

All eyes were upon us. All except Tommy's of course; they were hidden behind the white hat that was subtly blending into the white skin. Frankly, I didn't actually see Tommy's eyes until much later that day. At first, I thought this was an elaborate joke. Film professionals often have twisted senses of humor. But, no... this was no joke. This was some kind of Andy Warhol-esque reality. And, let's not forget I was "relaxing" in my pool a scant two hours previously (margaritas and such...). Raphael made the first move. He slowly reached over, pushed up on my jaw to close my mouth, pulled the invoice out of my hand, crumpled it up and punted it to the counter guy. The crumpled invoice bounced off the man's forehead...

I promised I would tell you the truth. I'm NOT exaggerating! The 10-12 thick-skinned, veteran filmmakers in that room simply could not quite believe what they were seeing. Neither could I. Jesus... this guy made Alice Cooper look like the poster child for normal. And, that was before he spoke...

Tommy shuffled toward me with his unique, sleep-walking gait. Raphael introduced us and carefully positioned himself behind Tommy's shoulder and faced me. I could see Raphael's face... Tommy could not. And then it happened. I heard Tommy speak for the first time... eyeballs in that room started flickering around looking for reassurance they weren't imagining things... feet began inching forward in search of a proper vantage point for the upcoming show... and, you just knew there would be a show. Given the peculiarities of the setting, a show was as inevitable as gravity. My eyes slowly rotated to Raphael. His face was split with a grin and his head was bobbing exactly like the Freud bobble-head that sits on my kitchen counter.

I fixed my gaze at a point on Tommy's hat where his eyes ought to be and girded my loins for battle. I wasn't quite hooked... yet. Our conversation began. And, please, for the full effect of this conversation, to the best of your ability, you must read Tommy's lines with his accent. I know this isn't easy...

T: Raphael says I need you to make my movie. Why? What do you do?
S: I'm a script supervisor.
T: What's that?

Uh-oh, not good... Raphael shrugged his shoulders and raised his eyebrows. Okay. I'll play along. I spent the next ten minutes explaining the skills and duties of a script supervisor. The older veterans in the room were quietly explaining some of the finer points for the younger kids. Raphael continued to wear his smug smile and bob his head. And for me? The light was beginning to dawn. Tommy responded to my explanation.

T: Ohhhhh... That's good. We need that.

I heard a few quickly silenced snickers from around the room. These guys are only human. They simply couldn't help themselves. Tommy is completely oblivious; and, yes... I am now hooked. Whatever it takes, whatever I have to do, whatever sacrifice I must make... I have got to share this man with the universe. Raphael is grinning and bobbing... and looking quite smug.

S: Yes, you do need that. I'm sure I can help you here.

This may be the single, largest understatement I have ever uttered in my entire life.

T: Could you also tell the actors what to do and yell "Action" and "Cut" and tell the
Cameraman what shots to get and figure out where the actors go in the scenes…

Say what?! I'm standing here in a damp Hawaiian shirt and he said, what?! No matter how surreal and bizarre my work experiences have been heretofore, this was fresh territory. A hush falls over the audience…

S: Umm… You want me to direct your project?
T: NO! I am Director!

The room erupts in snickering and quickly silences. Tommy is oblivious. Seriously, he was completely oblivious to every person and noise in that room. Of course, the hat was covering his eyes so it was hard to tell… Raphael is grinning and bobbing.

S: Yeah. You're the Director. Whatever. You want me to direct your movie or not?!
T: Yes, please.

The room erupts in laughter and quickly silences. Tommy is oblivious. And, behind Tommy, Raphael was grinning from ear to ear, bobbing his head and had his hands clasped together as he silently mouthed the words, "Please, please, please, please, please." By all that's holy, how could I possibly resist?!

[By the way, I know this conversation has been reprinted

in countless articles in the media. This conversation happened exactly as I wrote it. These are the words. This is the truth.]

Still, I am a professional and certain details must be worked out.

S: Okay. How much are you going to pay me?
T: I will pay you $75 per day.
The room erupts with screaming laughter. The counter guy is having apoplexy. Raphael is grinning and bobbing. Tommy is oblivious.

S: Dude, that's what I pay my pool man. Raphael, thanks for the call. I'll see you later.

I start to walk out.

T: NO! Wait! How much do you want?!
S: Add a zero to that number and we'll talk.
T: Oh my God! So much?!

The room erupts with laughter. The counter guy has to sit down. Naturally, the entire room was privy to our negotiations. I had a captive audience who couldn't believe what they were seeing. That's fair. I couldn't believe what I was seeing either.

I really need to stress that Tommy was completely unaware of the absolute absurdity of this surreal moment... and, for ALL the moments that came after.

T: Okay. I will pay.
S: It's a deal. When do you want to start shooting this project?

Tommy looks at his watch and from somewhere under his hat I hear...
T: In half hour.

The room came unglued... Cameramen are peeing themselves. The counter guy has slipped into a laughter induced coma. I've never seen Raphael this happy. He knows I'm hooked and he knows I'm here for the duration.

S: Okay... sure. Uhh... Raphael?

Raphael, my friend and boon companion, wearing a smug smile and with tears sliding down his aging, wrinkled cheeks, flings open the back door of the Birns & Sawyer Prep Room and there, spread out around the rear parking lot is a complete low-budget film crew and piles of equipment. I make eye contact with Raphael... and he stares into my brain. We carry on an entire conversation in those few seconds. Oh yeah, I'm hooked.
S: Okay... sure. Uhh... Tommy? Where are my actors?

Tommy points out five youngsters and one oldster sitting off to the side. Most of my wonderful cast had no acting experience whatsoever. They were, however, filled with passion and enthusiasm; and frankly, passion and enthusiasm is enough. The rest is just details...

S: Okay... sure. Uhh... Tommy? Where's my script?

Tommy hands me 3 pages. That's right. 3 pages. I never had a script. I was never given a script! All I ever had were a few pages at a time. "Is Genius, Sandy!" Yeah... is genius... if you're the only man in the asylum. Occasionally, when I have long hard days on actual film sets, I think about "The Room" and my mood always lightens. Let me finish the hiring process and then we'll talk about my nonexistent script.

S: Okay... sure. Uhh... Raphael? Where the Hell are we going to shoot this?

Raphael walks me around to the back of Birns & Sawyer where, lo-and-behold, there is a tiny, minuscule, microscopic stage. This stage was about the size of... wait for it... a room. Ahh... the light dawns! Tommy is going to shoot "The Room" in a room. Yep. Given what I had already seen on that surreal day, it actually made sense.
This is all I had to shoot with in terms of locations, one tiny stage and the Birns &Sawyer parking lot. All of the equipment, wardrobe, make-up and set dressing were stored on stage at night – no easy task, I assure you. The following morning, we would unlock the stage and everything would be jostled back out to the parking lot. I would then quickly dress the stage according to my interpretation of Tommy's pages; and, the madness would begin anew.

Tommy had purchased a million dollars' worth of equipment, a crew and a cast... but, he had no fucking idea what to do with it. "I am Director!" Yeah, sure you are. Sorry, Dude. You can't buy experience. It's simply not for sale.

My friends, I had indeed fallen down the rabbit hole; and, there was no returning to reality until my adventure was over... or my paychecks didn't clear.

CHAPTER 4

MY APPROACH

The worst film ever made? Hardly. If "The Room" was the worst film ever made, nobody would have ever heard of it, nor would anybody ever remember it. This film has millions of fans who have seen this movie so many times they know the dialogue and action by heart. "The Room" has qualities that have endeared it to film fans the world over. Where did those qualities come from? Who put them in this film? It takes more than just one quirky actor to make a film successful.

A Director works with the materials at hand. The materials I had on "The Room" were bizarre, strange, surreal, and weird. When you add an inexperienced crew and cast to the mixture along with absence of a script, the challenge becomes extreme and unique. I knew if I couldn't find some sort of cohesive pattern this film really would become the worst film ever made.

Regardless of whether you're making the next "Star Wars" movie or your next student film, you need to formulate an approach. Like most Hollywood veterans, I've worked on features of every size, budget and length. You must face every project with some sort of overall plan or you'll be doomed to failure. The final film will not even be watchable. In general, the larger the budget, the longer the schedule, the easier it is to formulate a plan and a schedule and <u>stick with it</u>.

Small projects like "The Room" can be very difficult in terms of an approach. It was an uphill battle from the beginning. I was handcuffed at every turn and the obstacles placed in my path were nearly overwhelming. They were also funny as Hell. By the way, surmounting overwhelming obstacles can be a lot of fun.

Most veterans in Hollywood have spent their entire careers observing untalented filmmakers wasting millions of dollars making crap while they "lived the dream." When Tommy hired me to direct "The Room," he handed me the largest "Crap" project I'd ever seen. "Crap" is a genre. It's a genre that civilians rarely get to see and one that film professionals are all too familiar with. I was driven to make this film the finest example of Crap I could. I needed an approach that would give it a chance to get noticed.

Given the nature and inexperience of the beast, I had to make my approach as simple as I possibly could or we would never finish the scenes, the days or, ultimately, the project itself. I went for a 1950's melodrama approach. In other words, plenty of dialogue delivered in profile and long Master Shots with minimal coverage to cut during editing. This simple approach works. If you think this doesn't work on "real" movies, I suggest you take a look at "Rebel without a Cause." The pivotal dramatic scene in this film is staged on the stairs with James Dean, Jim Backus and Ann Doran. James Dean pleads with his father to finally stand up for himself and "be a man." This entire scene is one long Master Shot without coverage being cut into it. The scene is carried along by nothing more than the brilliant dialogue of Stewart Stern and the even more brilliant talent of the actors.

Yes... I lacked "Rebel's" script, cast, crew, equipment, schedule, locations, and craft service; but, I could still learn from it and plunge ahead. You do not survive in the film business by giving up before you start. You must always exercise your ambition and creativity. You must be a pit bull. You must persevere, conquer your challenges, surmount your obstacles, and simply do the best you can with what you have.

Mentally, on "The Room," I wanted to hear the downbeat of a church organ at the end of every scene. You know, "dah-dah-DAH!" Ultimately, the goal was to get through the material efficiently, safely and with nobody getting permanent brain damage.

You can't just walk into that tiny, minuscule stage at Birns & Sawyer and hope the film will shoot itself. You have to have a plan! Tommy hired me and I had to have a plan; and, I had to come up with that plan as fast as I could. After all, I had an entire crew and cast waiting for me to issue orders and start shooting. And, I'm still wearing my damp Hawaiian shirt. I walked onto that microscopic stage with Raphael and closed the door. We looked at the space... we looked at each other... we cracked up laughing... and Raphael put on his cameraman hat and asked his Director exactly what he's supposed to ask his Director, "So... how do you want to do this?" He laughed as he said it, but he really did need an answer... and his 17 days were only just starting. I was well and truly caught between the proverbial rock and the Tommy.

My mind went into hyper drive. I had to come up with an approach, and I had to come up with it ten minutes ago. Normally (a word never applied to this project), a

Director has months, if not years, to formulate an approach. I knew I had to keep it simple. We lacked the material, script, cast and crew for anything complicated. I'm a big fan of Nicholas Ray, and an even bigger fan of "Rebel without a Cause." This film is teen angst at its best and I'm intimately familiar with Nicholas Ray's approach. It's simple, straight-forward and as uncomplicated as it gets. We would either use this approach or we would use nothing. I was out of options.

Guess what? It worked.

Every single conversation, interview or lecture I've ever given regarding "The Room" has always contained the exact same question. "Why on earth would you want credit for directing the WORST film ever made?" Well, excuse the fuck out of me! The worst film ever made?! Not hardly! You've never heard of the worst film ever made. Nobody has. Believe me, there are millions of "worst films ever made." They are all sitting in cans or lying on hard drives gathering dust in countless basements all over the world. Their Directors are washing dishes in Peoria.

I know, beyond a shadow of doubt, with 100% certainty, every veteran film professional reading these words is nodding their head with complete understanding and agreement.

There is an old adage in Hollywood that is as true now as it was when it was first uttered on some obscure silent film set. Many, if not most, folks in this industry will wish you success... just so long as your success is not more than theirs. Certainly, there are exceptions. I would like to think that I am an honorable exception to this rule. As stupid as it sounds on this page, I have always tried to live with a code of honor and ethics. The key to surviving Hollywood is to surround yourself with like-minded, trustworthy colleagues and coworkers. I would trust my industry friends with my life... and do so frequently.

I met Tommy Wiseau and was handed an opportunity. This is Hollywood... and opportunities are few and far between. directing opportunities are even fewer and farther between. The only way you can advance yourself in this ruthless business – this business that I love – is almost always by your own initiative. As I stated previously, this business is not for the weak or faint of heart.

Tommy handed me an opportunity and I did my very best with it. I could so easily have simply put in my time, mailed in my job performance, cashed my checks and moved on to another gig when this one ended. In this town, you are what you make of yourself.

According to most critics, my approach to the materials I had to work with got "The Room" noticed... by the entire English speaking world. "The Room" was a complete success any way you want to measure it.
For 14 long years... every single time Tommy Wiseau knowingly lies and claims he Directed "The Room," he steals this success from me. Every article, every interview, every radio and television broadcast that backs up Tommy's outrageous claim steals this success from me.

I am so completely tired of these lies... right down to the bone tired... I have kept a low profile for 14 years; but, enough is enough!

For better or worse, I am the Director of "The Room."

CHAPTER 5

THE SCRIPT?

Tommy handed me 2 or 3 pages on that first day and every subsequent day thereafter… with <u>no page numbers</u>… <u>with no slug lines</u> (exterior or interior, scene location, time of day)… and, <u>no action descriptions</u>; except, of course, constantly throwing the football at each other from five feet away and almost murdering Denny on the roof for drugs and money. Basically, all I had was character names and garbled, unintelligible dialogue. I had absolutely no idea what the characters were doing. This was true for the entire project! I never had a script. Let me repeat that so there is no confusion whatsoever. **<u>THERE WAS NO SCRIPT!</u>**

On January 2, 2016, I celebrated my new year by watching a two minute video that Tommy uploaded on YouTube in an asinine and idiotic attempt to prove that I had a full script prior to shooting. As usual, this is a pile of bullshit! This is one of the reasons why I felt compelled to write this book. This guy keeps bashing me online and in countless articles and interviews. What would you do? I'll tell you what you'd do. You'd sit down and start writing a book.

I would like to point out that Tommy makes my case for me. The video is filled with little circles around little stapled pages. These stapled pages are the 2 and 3 page bits of idiocy I was handed when I finished working on the previous 2 or 3 page bits of idiocy. Go ahead, watch the video a few times; which is probably a few times more than Tommy watched it. Every highlighted circle (except one) shows the cast and crew reading a few pages that have been stapled together. These were my daily script pages. In the words of the immortal bard, 3 pages stapled together do not a script make! I sound a little pissed off right now because I am a little pissed off right now. I get so damn tired and irritated every time Tommy gets a bug up his ass and decides to lie and smear me on YouTube. It's irritating and annoying. Just because I've never responded to Tommy's lies and insinuations during the past 14 years doesn't mean I won't write a book someday and set the record straight. Oh wait a second...

Tommy does show one nearly completed script in his little video upload. The script in the video is the script that was in my bag and this script was ONLY completed on the last day of shooting! You'll have to take my word for it that this script is incomplete. Tommy was handing me a couple of pages at a time; and, with a few exceptions, they were in chronological story order. In other words, in terms of the story (what story?), the script pages that he was doling out to me followed the previous scene's pages in uninterrupted story time.

Nearly all movies made are shot out of sequence. For example, you shoot all the scenes that occur at a specific location and then you move on to a new location. You never want to revisit a location you've already shot out. It's expensive, inefficient and stupid to return and relight a location after you've packed up and moved on to a new location -- expensive, inefficient and stupid... the Tommy Wiseau School of Filmmaking.

During the entire course of the project, when I finished shooting my pages, I would place them sequentially in my script book. Thus, the script would slowly grow each day. The script in my bag was the ONLY script marked up with notes for Post Production. The pages of the script in Tommy's little video upload are my marked up script pages! The film was going to be edited after we were done shooting it. What was I going to do, throw the pages away when I was done shooting them?! Of course not! I was keeping and maintaining the shooting pages and my notes for the editor to use when he cut the film together. As I finished my pages, I would add them to the pages already shot. The shooting script grew a few pages each day. Finally, on the last day of shooting, the script was complete... a script that didn't exist until the end of the project!

Don't forget, in addition to performing the duties of Director and 1st AD, I was also the script supervisor. One of the duties of a script supervisor is to make notes in the margins and inside the scripted dialogue that are used by the editors in Post Production to cut the film together. I never had a completed script to look at. Never! The one shot in Tommy's idiotic video that shows a full script (and my hand) is covered with my script and shooting notes in the margins. In other words, these marked up pages have already been shot on set! These are not script pages waiting to be shot. Wow, I feel just like Perry Mason.

Tommy has such a desperate need to convince the fans of "The Room" that he Directed the movie and wrote a complete script prior to shooting that he actually uploaded footage to You Tube that shows me directing on set. Just look for the Hawaiian shirt floating around in the background. That's right! He uploaded footage of me directing on set in order to prove he wrote the script prior to shooting. Desperate acts tend to create embarrassing contradictions, don't they?

Each day, Tommy or Greg would hand me two to four pages. When I finished my pages, I would get a few more pages. I had absolutely no idea what was coming at me next. No idea whatsoever! (Oh look, a rooftop in San Francisco! How the fuck am I going to pull this off?! I know, I'll just pull a brick rooftop out of my ass... which I keep in my large colon right next to the furniture. Lunacy!) These are unique challenges any film Director would wince at. I have no idea where the story begins or stops or ends. No idea who the protagonists or antagonists are. No idea as to the emotional temperature and flow of the story.

I had nothing... nothing but fun! I have always loved puzzles. "The Room" was the most entertaining puzzle I've ever solved. Regardless of how stupid and pointless a project may seem – and "The Room" was about as stupid and pointless as filmmaking gets -- a Director still has to shoot it in such a fashion that it can be cut together by the editor in Post Production. That's the job. Film Directors do this, not egocentric liars who feel they must get credit for every job performed on set.

Occasionally, if I finished my pages in a timely fashion – timely according to Tommy – he would stuff a $20 in my shirt pocket. Yes, my friends, I got tips... I didn't know whether to laugh or cry...

After I finished my daily allotment of pages, if there was still time left in my shooting day... I would get a couple more pages to direct. Naturally, the new pages rarely had anything even remotely in common with the pages I had just finished directing; nor were there action or location descriptions. I simply crafted a spot on set to stage the action and then figure out a way to somehow make it relate to the footage already shot. Whether or not I could succeed at this was a crap shoot and completely in the hands of God. Tommy would then endlessly repeat, "Make sure Denny has his football." Oh, for fuck's sake... Why?! Why?! Why?!

For example: There is this absolutely fragmented, discombobulated scene toward the end of the movie with Peter the Psychologist, Mark the Cheater and Tommy/Johnny. We learn: Lisa is probably cheating, love is blind, Mark might have a new girlfriend (nudge, nudge) and Peter doesn't want to run the Bay-To-Breakers race; whatever the Hell that is – "cheep, cheep, cheep." (This is how grown men tease each other in "The Room." They call each other chicken and go "cheep, cheep, cheep." Priceless...) Tommy then goes to the kitchen (What kitchen?! That's the bathroom door! Whatever...), and Lisa and Denny walk in and have a short conversation squatting on the floor behind a chair near the front door. Weird, right? Okay. See, Tommy didn't really go to the kitchen or the bathroom. He left the set to get a page of dialogue he wanted to add to the scene... the scene we just finished shooting... and, the new page is with Lisa and Denny... in the scene we JUST – FINISHED - SHOOTING! Say what?! Who?! How? Reshoot the scene? Draw them in digitally? I can't. I have neither the time nor the VFX personal to make this happen. How? I'll tell you how. I simply pivoted the lights from the couch to the door, flipped the camera 180 degrees on its axis, and brought Lisa and Denny onto the set. Then, I had them sit on the floor next to the door for their pointlessly inane, melodramatic moment. Why would I do this, you ask? Because the doorway was already lit and that stage was a tiny fucking box, that's why! I had already shot every square inch of that stage and it was the only place I hadn't shot yet -- the floor behind the chair next to the door. It was absurd and stupid and matched the dialogue. In other words... perfect.

The dialogue constantly referred to characters and subplots NOT included in the story line... and then never mentioned again. It was like having an acid trip. My world had dissolved into fragmented sentences, fragmented scenes, fragmented subplots and fragmented conversations with Tommy Wiseau. The man doesn't really speak in complete sentences.

I always expected Rod Serling to step out from behind a curtain with a half-smoked cigarette dangling between his fingers and add narration to the filming process, "Submitted for your approval..." Remember, I had no prior knowledge of what would be contained on the day's pages. It was cinematic Russian roulette... being played in a minefield. I had to be light on my feet... bobbing and weaving... dancing to the beat of Rod Serling's tune... and somehow convey a coherent plan to my cast and crew.

You think the dialogue is bad now?! Oh, no, no, no, no... At least now, when you watch the film, you can actually understand what the actors are saying. When the pages first came off Tommy's typewriter – I always pictured him hacking away at a 1929 Underhill typewriter with a loud bell and a carriage return – the pages were nearly unintelligible. I'm being completely honest here. The pages had no grammar, no structure – you know, adjective-noun-adverb-verb – and the words frequently made no sense at all, "But, Mom, houseplant growing running bookcase flower, Johnny!" Okay... Genius! When the pages were given to the actors, they would descend on me as if I was a quarterback kneeling on a muddy field in the middle of a football huddle; fighting for our lives late in the fourth quarter. They would begin chanting their mantra, "Please, Sandy, for the love of God, rewrite this so it makes sense!" Bless their hearts... they weren't concerned that the dialogue was beyond ridiculous and made absolutely no sense whatsoever... they just wanted sentences that could be understood by other human beings.

The trick, you see, was to rewrite and tweak the dialogue so Tommy wouldn't notice. "Is Genius, Sandy!" Yeah... you bet... I needed to keep his dramatic intent (such as it was...) and, at the same time, have it make some sort of sense... in English... spoken as it is in the 21st century. Tommy would, of course, sporadically catch me rewriting the dialogue... and the shit would hit the proverbial fan! Naturally, this would only happen on the days he was on set "acting." Otherwise, I had free rein. It usually went something like this: "No! Don't touch the words! They are genius!" I replied with my standard, "These words make no sense!" We would argue... we would get pissed at each other... I would go sit in my car... Tommy would knock on my window... I would roll it down one inch... and Tommy would offer me more money to get out of my car and go back to work... which I would have done anyway, if I wasn't having so much fun getting a small raise in my daily salary. This scenario played out repeatedly; and, I loved each and every bizarre, surreal, melodramatic moment of it. Oh, c'mon… wouldn't you? If I got Tommy really pissed off, his white face would actually develop some color. Score!

I couldn't wait to get my new pages every day. It was like opening a Kinder Egg and discovering an eerie, bizarre, mutated prize inside. There were university textbooks I read while I was studying psychology that were not nearly as entertaining or insightful as the exceedingly cryptic pages I got from Tommy.

Submitted for your approval: Mom's first husband Harold – Mom's breast cancer – Mom divorcing Edward (who the Hell is Edward?!) – those 'fuckers' at work – Mark's ex-girlfriend Betty (Betty? What, no Veronica?) – Denny loves Lisa, but will marry Elizabeth. Who are these people?! Who the Hell is Elizabeth?! I suppose if I had cutaway vignettes like they have on "Family Guy" it might have made more sense, but… c'est la vie.

Mom has breast cancer?! Are you fucking kidding me?! Breast cancer?!
I did manage to corner Tommy and point out, "Tommy, dude… breast cancer is NOT funny! Breast cancer is serious!" He responded in typical Tommy fashion, "Sandy, I know that… I know breast cancer is serious… This is a very serious scene." I ask you, how do you argue with logic like that? Mom sandwiches her breast cancer confession between Harold the Jerk wanting her house

and her joy at having divorced Edward. Lisa responds by claiming Tommy hit her! What? He did? When? Aha! That bastard! You just have to go with it...

To be quite honest, the Mother/Daughter conversations were my favorite. I always tried to shoot them in such a way as to mirror the absurdity of the content. I especially liked their conversation during Johnny's birthday party when Mom says, "You should marry Johnny; you need financial security. Don't throw your life away just because you don't love him. All men are assholes. I never wanted to marry your father." Alrighty then... sound motherly advice.

We walk into the apartment and a couple of new characters, Michelle and Mike, are smearing chocolate on their faces and making out on the couch. Why? Why? Why? Because Tommy, my Producer, said the scene was critical to the script and the story, and I had to shoot it, that's why. Okay... let's see if I can make this work... without damaging anyone's psyche permanently. Furthermore, Mike has to leave his boxer's behind. Right... this happens all the time... Men all over the world are able to pull their pants on and simply not notice they've forgotten to put on their underwear. Really? I'm a man. I tend to notice when my pecker is being chaffed by denim. If you are not a man, ask any man nearby. I'm sure he'll back me up on this.

Phrases I repeated regularly on set: "What are these characters doing here?! Why does Johnny love Denny so much?! Why does he want to adopt him?" and, "Why, in the name of all that's holy and decent in the world does Tommy want me to always have him carrying a football?!!" Oh look, Rod Serling's back...
Truthfully, the relationship between Johnny and Denny

was the only part of the melodrama that had the hair on the back of my neck standing up. The character of Denny is that of a grown man. I was concerned that his relationship with Johnny was bordering on being inappropriate and I toned a lot of it down. Trust me, I really did. I wasn't there for the whole "I want to watch" pillow fight moment or I would have toned that down too. Still there was a lot... The movie starts with Denny wanting to join Johnny for a nap... And, how long has THAT been going on?

And, what about Johnny's best friend and his fiancée?! Mark and Lisa are exactly what they seem. They're both lying cheating sluts. Makes you kind of wonder what demons the screenwriter was exorcising on his script pages, doesn't it? Nope. Not going to go there...
Johnny and Lisa's relationship is about as dysfunctional as things get. I viewed their torturous and doomed love affair as sort of a Stanley Kowalski meets Wednesday Addams. She would have happily ripped Johnny's heart out of his chest and eaten it raw with nice Chianti and some fava beans. But first, she must destroy his mind and soul! The project started as "Days of our Lives" and evolved into "Dark Shadows." Of course, I never expected Barnabas Collins to have an emotional hissy fit and blow his brains out! That caught me a bit by surprise.

By the way, have you done the math? At the end of the movie, Tommy screams at Lisa, "I gave you seven years!" When did he start dating her? When she was 13? And, he yells it all through the bathroom door... no, the kitchen door... no, the bathroom door... I felt like the Keymaster in "Matrix."

Michelle and Mike are pretty straight forward. They're both into chocolate and sex. I did get a campy kick out of

Michelle's annoying use of the expression "XYZ" to tell Mark to zip up his pants. "Examine your zipper," she says shyly. Frankly, that's a lot of coy behavior from a woman who just had chocolate sex.

Mom is easy. She's just a merciless bitch.

The rest of the cast simply kept popping in and out of the pages randomly and completely without warning. Kept me light on my toes.

The Rooftop Scene... No. Not here. I think the Rooftop Scene should get its own chapter, don't you?

Each day I would be given fresh pages to shoot. The crew emptied the stage while I spent the first half hour in the morning with a cup of coffee in one hand, and the pages in the other – reading and re-reading the dialogue... trying to decipher the intent... trying to swallow my disbelief that I would actually shoot live actors saying these lines... and, of course, the endless cavalcade of new characters. New characters would appear out of nowhere, with no warning whatsoever, with no explanation. For example, Peter the Psychologist, who is obviously a bit of a chicken – "cheep, cheep, cheep" – because he doesn't want to play football while wearing a tuxedo. Even for "The Room" that was weird. Oh look, Rod's back. I just can't seem to keep him off the stage.

There was a line at the end of the movie when Tommy hustles everyone out the door and says, "There's too many weirdos here." Wow! The irony was so thick you could cut it with a dull plastic spoon.

Why are they playing football in tuxedos? Why? Why? Seriously, my friends, I have absolutely no idea why. It was a very last minute request from Tommy Wiseau... my producer. I will never get used to typing those words...

By the way, anybody who is reading this book and considering a career in film, you really need to understand this and take it to heart.

Your producer is paying the bills and your salary; therefore, your producer is in charge. Fighting this principal will bring about the demise of your career, and you too will wind up washing dishes in Peoria. You fulfill your producer's requests as best you can, regardless of whatever planet or dimension spits him out and places him on your plane of existence. You pick your battles and tuxedo clad football players is not one of them; your producer's mental acuity or his tenuous grasp of reality is completely irrelevant. Your producer is the boss – boss, not Director. Being the boss does not make you a film Director. Your producer tells you what he wants to achieve. Directors, cinematographers, designers, crew, and all the rest of us listed in those credits... we listen to our producers and attempt to fulfill their requests to the best of our ability. That's the game. Get used to it. Embrace it.

Where was I? Oh yeah, playing football in tuxedos. I think Tommy ordered the tuxedos for a wedding rehearsal scene that never materialized. The tuxedo/football scene was a very last minute, spontaneous request by Tommy. You know how it goes... "Hey, I have great idea," (Oh, God help me...), "Let's play football while we've got our tuxedos on." Naturally, one has to ask why? I mean, seriously, I had to ask. I'm the Director, the 1st AD, and the script supervisor. It's my job to ask. My loyal troops are looking at me for guidance. The answer? Wait for it... "Because that's what men do."

Aha! There it is! The answer to the riddle of the endless stream of footballs in this movie! Because real men carry footballs! Who knew?! I am now to assume Tommy Wiseau has his finger on the pulse of the American male. At this point during my trek through Wonderland, I felt that it was far simpler and safer to simply shoot the boys playing football in their tuxedos rather than question the rationale of the scene... with La Brea Boulevard in the background... and Birns & Sawyer's main entrance awning on the side of the frame. I thought that was pretty funny. Too bad nobody would ever get to see the movie when I finished it, right? You just never know when fate is going to throw a monkey wrench at your head.

Okay, tell me you didn't love the off-key rendition of "Happy Birthday Johnny" during the birthday party scene. I had to do a lot of takes... everyone was laughing. As for the birthday party itself, not even Rod Serling would have ventured into such uncharted waters. I even had Michelle and Mike play with their cake. You know, sort of in keeping with the whole food/sex theme. My favorite moment was when Lisa and Mark are kissing and they get busted by a character we've never seen before and we have absolutely no idea who he is. Don't forget, this is appearing at the end of the film; which is infinitely too late to be introducing new characters. He screams. He yells. He preaches. He gives advice. And, he ends with, "You make me sick!" What can I say? Tommy hands me the pages and I direct them. Naturally, I asked Tommy, "Who the Hell is the guy in the white shirt?!" Tommy's response? "He's one of Johnny's closest friends; but, wasn't in the rest of the film because he's been out of town." Really? That's the explanation? He's been out of town?! Out of town when? Out of town while we're shooting the movie? Out of town in the story? Out of town in reality? That's it! He's out of town in Tommy's reality. Okay... that makes sense... sure, why the Hell not? And, deeper into the rabbit hole we crawl... Hi, Rod!

"Hey everybody, we're expecting!" Oh shit... This isn't even in the scripted pages. Every head on set swiveled to me... for guidance... for leadership... I simply shrugged and embraced the moment. After all, I had been battling the Jabberwock for nearly one full month by this time. When Tommy stepped up on the apple box, with the cameras rolling, and announced that he and Lisa are expecting... Well... after nearly four weeks of shooting, it just all seemed kind of normal. Of course, in the ensuing scene, Lisa has a fabulous explanation for her pregnancy, "I said it to make it interesting." Interesting for whom? The Marquis de Sade?!

Then, the big fight at the birthday party... This scene, mixed into the morass of this cinematic narrative, never made any sense to me whatsoever and I was tired... So, I simply shot it as it was written; but, I kept changing the emotionality of the dialogue. The words stayed the same; but, I had the characters vary the emotionality. They're fighting... they're making up... they're fighting... they're making up... they're fighting...
Naturally, I had the actors happy, then sad, then happy, then sad... It was all so completely bizarre... and tons of fun! Nothing I had been shooting for the past month ever made any sense, so why should the birthday party be any different?

THEN, we finish it all by wrecking the set, pitching the television set off the roof of the sound stage, and Johnny kills himself. Classic film noir! My own personal theory is that Johnny shot himself so Tommy wouldn't write any more pages.

"Who wrote this crap!?"

We took dozens of publicity stills. This was Tommy's best smile...and, I could never figure out how to get him to open his eyes. Always the "Clint Eastwood" grimace and squint...

Tommy loved posing with the Zoolander pout...

"I see...a horrible sexual encounter in your future!"

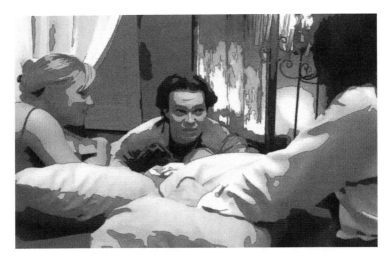

CHAPTER 6

THE SPOONS

The spoons! The spoons! Why do I feel like I'm channeling Quasimodo? I <u>must</u> explain the photos of the plastic spoons and give you the truth behind this little slice of insanity. No, really, I insist. The spoons are such an integral part of the "The Room" experience. I can't begin to tell you how much I've enjoyed watching how audiences have reacted to the photo of the spoons. Wow! Throwing plastic silverware at the movie screen! I love it!

I remember watching Tommy in an interview not too long ago, and he was pontificating about the origin of the spoons. He said: "Now in today's society you look at plastic spoons, look at how far we go, but at the same time, the symbolism to respond to your questions is, plastic is very harmful for you. If you look at the plastic that we make in America lets say 10 years ago compared to today, two different things. Today you can eat from plastic spoons and you will not get certain allergies for example. I'm familiar with that, why? Because I studied this. As you know I studied psychology.

So you know this is symbolism, also survival aswell. Think about it...this is one tiny little thing in The Room where people can connect together". Sigh... What a crock! Shear, unadulterated bullshit! I don't know whether to laugh or cry. He took something as innocent and ridiculous as the spoons and tried to spin it with depth. Like somehow, the spoons are philosophical and meaningful. Like the spoons were pre-planned. Nothing could be further from the truth.

Every time Tommy lies, an angel cries... yeah, cries with laughter. You would think someone who has so much practice at the art of fabrication would somehow have learned to do it better. Tommy has an ugly habit of explaining his reasons for doing something <u>long</u> after the 'something' has happened... like every time he tells his fans that he was directing a comedy. No, little man, I was making a comedy... you were making "Gone with the Wind" meets "Streetcar Named Desire." Naturally, he has an explanation – a complete fabrication – a ridiculous philosophical fairy tale – of how the spoons came to be on film.

For the life of me, I never saw this coming! Never in my wildest imagination could I have predicted how fans would react to the spoons! Who could? I <u>love</u> the spoons! I love the hilarity of an entire audience throwing plastic silverware at the screen!

A few years ago, I was working on "Supah Ninjas" for Nickelodeon. I really enjoyed working on this project. If you haven't seen any reruns, you should. The show was excellent! It was also really expensive, which is probably why it got canceled. We were shooting in Pittsburgh and I got a phone call from the owner of the Hollywood Theater.

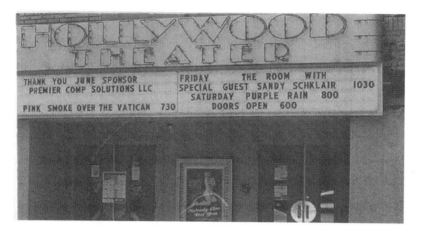

He said he plays "The Room" every Friday night, and would I please come by, introduce the movie and maybe answer a few questions from the small audience in attendance. Sure, why not? He failed to mention the small audience was about 2000 people. He also failed to mention he put my name on the marquis. Surprise! As payment, I asked him to save a row of seats for my "Supah Ninja" crew mates. This was the tail end of a 70 hour work week and my crew mates showed up in all manner of altered mental states – perfect for a "Room" viewing. Naturally, when we returned to work on Monday, I took a veritable mountain of crap for that evening's entertainment. I found plastic spoons tucked into my gear for months afterward. "Alright, who filled my podium with plastic spoons?!" Funny...

I gave a brief introduction to the movie and ended with a promise to answer any and all questions after the movie ended. I demanded the crowd find me a seat in the center of the theater and I joined the rowdy fans. What a blast! I screamed rude comments; I joined everyone in shouting, "You are tearing me apart, Lisa!" I threw spoons -- "SPOONS!" And, a wonderful time was had by all; a truly beautiful Friday night. When the film ended, I walked to the front of the auditorium and answered questions. There were so many spoons on the floor it was like walking on bubble wrap – pop pop pop pop pop pop pop. Hilarious! I explained the spoons…

I had a teeny-tiny stage with the teeny-tiny living room set. As you may recall, there were two chairs with an empty table between them. I staged a large number of conversations in those chairs. I make no excuses for the set, you use what you have. And, I had two chairs and an empty table. I had the 1st AD (me) yell (walkie-talkie) to the Art Department (two youngsters eating burgers) to give me a prop for the table.

Me: Quick, give me something for the empty table. I want to roll the camera.

Art: We don't have anything!

Me: Whaddya mean you don't have anything? Give me your burger!

Art: We don't have anything suitable for the table.

Me: Suitable?! Is this your first day?!

Art: I got nothing that would go on a living room table. It wouldn't look right!

I just love the passion and dedication of youth… misguided though it is.

Me: Don't tell me what you don't have; tell me what you do have.

Art: All we have are these photo frames with the stupid marketing photos in them!

Me: Photos of what?!

Art: Plastic spoons. We don't have any real photos. It won't make any sense!

Me: Seriously?! This is your concern?! This doesn't make sense to you?!

Art: But, they're marketing photos.

Me: Nobody is going to care about the spoons! Just put them on the table!

Art: But...

Me: Just put the fucking frames on the table!

And that, as they say, is that. The marketing photos of plastic spoons landed on the table and I started shooting. The camera operator was swinging the camera between the characters and pushed in on the spoons as a joke... a joke for me as I watched the shot on my monitor. That's it, just a joke. From tiny little acorns do mighty oaks grow...

Cavemen? Metaphors? Are you fucking kidding me? It was a joke between the camera operator and me! No depth. No philosophy. I was watching the shot on the monitor and I laughed my ass off. He pushed into the spoons a few more times. It was funny! That's it! There's nothing more to it; no metaphor, no cavemen, no depth, no philosophy. It was just a fucking joke!

Who the Hell knew the editor would cut the spoons into the final print?!

CHAPTER 7

THE ALLEY, THE ROOFTOP AND THE PSYCHOLOGY OFFICE

Johnny: First, we need a word or two about the lead character, Johnny; the sensitive, tragically deep, angst-ridden hero of our little opus. I confess, the single greatest challenge for me in directing Tommy was getting him to enunciate his words so we could hear each and every savory gem roll off his tongue; and, getting him to open his eyes wider. I told him repeatedly that the "squint" only works well for Clint Eastwood and Charles Bronson. It's important... nay, critical... to remember that there is a lot of Johnny inside of Tommy. Honestly, unless Tommy is the greatest method actor since Marlon Brando, Tommy IS Johnny. They are one and the same. I couldn't have separated Tommy from Johnny with a legion of Grips all armed with jack hammers and crow bars. I assure you, when dealing with Tommy/Johnny, one needed to be flexible and fast on one's feet.

Three days into the project, I received serious insight into Tommy's unique approach to sex during the drunk/pizza eating scene I staged on the couch. When I asked Tommy to lean over and gently kiss Lisa on the cheek he... he... Sorry, I just can't go there. Let's just say that what I saw on the monitor was so mind-numbing and shocking that I screamed "CUT," washed my eyes out with bleach, recited three "Our Father's," and four "Hail Mary's." And, I'm Jewish for fuck's sake! Let's just say, in that moment, I saw enough of Tommy's tongue to last me several lifetimes! My sensibilities were shattered, and this was just a gentle kiss on the cheek. I believe I said something like "Dude, the next time I see your tongue on camera, I'm going to chop it off!" The writing was on the wall... NO love scenes with Tommy without rules and boundaries. **I will not direct pornography!**

Later that evening, after we wrapped, I asked Tommy how many love scenes he was going to write for himself. He enthusiastically told me he would have two <u>nude</u> love scenes with Lisa. I immediately told him, "Here in Hollywood, we always save love scenes for the last day of shooting... when the lead actors are most comfortable with one another." This may not strictly be true; but, what the Hell would you have done? And, yes, I resigned on the last day of shooting. Again, I ask you, what the Hell would you have done?!

<u>The Mugging In The Alley</u>: "Where's my money, Denny?! Where's my fucking money?! Where's my fucking money?!!!!!" Wowzers! Oh man, this scene's got everything! Action, drama, drugs, guns, bad guys, good guys, footballs (footballs?)! Oh yeah. This is gonna be good. I've gotta make this BIG! I've gotta make it HUGE! How fun is this?! Can you imagine? I was going to have anecdotes to tell on every film set I walk onto for the rest of my life! The only problem being, of course, getting future crews to believe this really happened and that I wasn't making it all up.

Our wonderful villain was played by Dan Janjigian, a really sweet guy and a reasonably talented actor. He actually kinda, sorta almost made it work... whatever the

Hell IT was. I placed the actors and blocked out the shot. We rehearsed it a couple of times. And... needless to say, Take 1 went south in a hurry! Thank God the gun wasn't loaded. The actors were all screaming at once, they all missed their marks and fell out of the light and onto the floor in a large pile-up, the camera operator was giggling with his eyes closed, Raphael was shrieking with laughter and looked like he might have a heart attack; and me? I was in fucking heaven! Better than Disneyland! Priceless! It simply does NOT get any better than this!

That was a fun scene to shoot and the actors really got into it; although, I'm not sure what, if anything it had to do with the story... if only I knew what the actual story was. Drugs? What drugs? What money? Should I have them stomp on Dan? Oh yeah, definitely another Rod Serling/Family Guy moment. And, why the Hell is there a villain in the alley?! How did he get there? Does he live in the building? Does he live in the neighborhood? Does Denny play football with him on the weekends? What? What? What?

This scene has one purpose and one purpose only. This unexpected, astonishing, out-of-the-blue, trite little piece of melodramatic mayhem gave Tommy – no, I mean Johnny... no wait... Tommy... Johnny... God, I'm so confused... This scene gave Tommy/Johnny a chance to play the hero and "come to the rescue." That is the only purpose of this scene. Mental masturbation at its finest; and, on film no less. So, what the Hell... I can do this. We'll have a huge guy with a gun the size of a Sherman Tank scare the crap out of Denny; and, Tommy/Johnny can come to the rescue and save the day... and, give Denny back his beloved football.

Days like this always threatened my view of reality;

which is why I loved days like this. I thoroughly reveled in the moment when Denny screams, "You're not my fucking Mother!!" That line is a cinematic Haley's comet… once around the sun with minimal damage and destruction, and then mercifully gone for another 72 years.

<u>Hitting Her and Saying "Hi Mark"</u>: "I did not hit her! I did nahht! Oh, hi Mark." Oh, Mama! Oscar here I come! I know just where I can get a slightly used tuxedo…

This is arguably the funniest and most memorable scene in the movie. Most of the hilarity of this scene is due to the fact that Tommy/Johnny was playing this as if he was Brando in "Street Car Named Desire." Deadly serious… and, caused a lot of retakes because my camera operator was laughing so hard he had trouble keeping the camera steady. Frankly, who can blame him? Take 1 was so insane the entire crew ended up laughing on the sound track, including me! I still have dailies from this scene. I play it every Halloween and giggle uncontrollably…

Let's examine the dialogue, shall we? "I did not hit her. I did nahht." I did nahht, what? Did not what? What? Could you <u>please</u> try and talk in complete sentences! Hit her… Hit who, for God's sake? Hit who? Hit Lisa? I know Lisa lied to her Mother and told her Tommy hit her; but, I have no clue how Tommy/Johnny found out. That was just a few scenes earlier. Since then, I had Mike and Michelle covered in chocolate, a missing pair of boxers, a drug dealer with a howitzer and a boatload of crying. I have no hitting or discussion of hitting. There is no past, present or future hitting. There is no hitting. What the Hell is Tommy/Johnny talking about? I thought maybe I might have missed something. After all, these are new pages. I quietly asked Greg, "Hit who, Dude?" His response was a wild-eyed smirk and a shrug of the shoulders. Definitely time to go with the flow. If you fight the logic, it only hurts more.

As I mentioned earlier, all I had to work with on this project was a single, tiny, one-room stage and a small portion of the Birns & Sawyer parking lot. As per our usual procedure, I found out about the rooftop scenes at the very last moment. Not a problem. The Grips set up a monochromatic green wall, which the salesmen at Birns & Sawyer were only too happy to sell us. (Cha-ching! Beach house!) We threw a small brick wall in front of the green screen, added a small rooftop doorway and, voila, a San Francisco rooftop. More or less... If only the CGI guys had been consistent with the background plates, it would have worked... although, I have to admit, it is infinitely funnier with the background discontinuity. I love that! The buildings keep shifting around. Hilarious!

A word about second unit work: All first unit Directors tend to worry a bit about the continuity of their second unit footage. Second unit Directors head off into the hinterlands with their hearty crews and shoot footage that has to be cut into First Unit footage. This has been getting screwed up ever since D.W. Griffith shot "Birth of a Nation." The second unit footage on "The Room" was pretty screwed up; but honestly, I really have seen worse. For example: After the "Oh, Hi Mark" scene on the roof, Lisa is sitting on the couch with Michelle and lying about Johnny hitting her; and Tommy enters the apartment empty handed. Second unit shot Tommy in San Francisco picking up his newspaper and walking upstage through the door. Mistakes like this happen on a lot of films. (Although, certainly <u>never</u> on any film when I'm in charge of continuity! Really... I swear...)
Seriously though, if the second unit Director (who?) had bothered to call me, we would have discussed his shots

and made sure they would be usable rather than being stupid and ridiculous. On the other hand, stupid and ridiculous really does work for "The Room."

The Scene: It was fairly straight-forward really... who knew it would take an entire day? All I needed was to stuff Tommy into the rooftop doorway set piece, yell "ACTION!" and, Bobs-your-uncle, Tommy would step out of the doorway, say the magic words, "I did not hit her. I did not," look up, see Greg, and say, "Hi Mark." You would think this would be simple, no? Perhaps in your universe this is simple... However, here in the Twilight Zone, even 'simple' can be an exotic adventure. And through the Looking Glass we went...

Take 1: ACTION! Tommy opens the door, takes a step, slams his head into the transom over the door and practically knocks himself unconscious. Holy shit, I never saw that coming. CUT! I choke back the laughter, get a very wobbly Tommy to his feet, apply make-up to the crease in his forehead; and, stuff Tommy back into the doorway.

Take 2: ACTION! Tommy opens the door, slams his head into the transom, and once again knocks himself to the ground. CUT! Unbelievable! If I hadn't seen it with my own eyes... On all subsequent takes, including the one cut into the finished film, you can see Tommy eyeballing the transom as he steps through. Not kidding. So... we stuff Tommy back inside the doorway and try again.

Take 3: ACTION! Tommy walks through the door, gives the transom the stink-eye and says, "I did not – Sandy?!" CUT! "Yeah, Tommy, what's up?" Tommy replies, "I am mad. I must throw something." Aha! I get a wee bit more insight into Tommy's personality. I grab a water bottle from a passing PA and hand it to Tommy, "Here, throw this." And, we stuff Tommy back inside the doorway.

Take 4: ACTION! Tommy walks through the door, gives the transom the stink-eye, drinks from the water bottle with the cap still on, shouts "I did not hit her! I did not!" and hurls the water bottle... knocking a large planter off the wall. CUT! I had to cut the shot. Not only was the set covered with planter shards and dirt; but, the crew was laughing all over the sound track. Tommy, of course, was seriously immersed in channeling Marlon Brando and remained oblivious to the comedy of errors. Okay... We cleaned the set, replaced the planter, gave Marlon a fresh water bottle and stuffed him back inside the doorway.

Take 5: ACTION! Tommy walks through the door, gives the transom the stink-eye, shouts, "I did not hit her! I did not!" hurls the water bottle, says, "Oh, hi Mark," and then looks up at Greg, who is sitting off camera. CUT! I patiently explain, "Tommy, Dude, you need to look up, actually see Mark with your own eyes, and then say, 'Oh, hi Mark.' You have to see him before you can say hi to him. Otherwise, it will look silly..." (Yeah. I know.) And, we stuff Tommy back inside the doorway.

Take 6: ACTION! Suffice to say, Takes 6-20 did not work. Things broke... Tommy tripped over the dolly track... people got hurt... mayhem and madness ensued... and, I just couldn't get Tommy to look up before he said howdy to his good buddy Mark. I needed to think about this...
"That's lunch everybody! One half-hour!"

While the crew was at lunch, I placed pieces of tape at the far end of the set where Mark would be sitting. Tommy's eye line to the tape would appear on camera as if he was looking at Mark. After lunch, we stuffed Tommy back inside the doorway in preparation for the next take. I quickly placed a large, spry Grip upstage next to the tape and told him to duck down out of sight, "Okay, dude, here's the plan. When you hear Tommy deliver his 'I did naahhht!' I want you to jump into the air and yell!" I ran back behind the camera and crossed my fingers.

Take Whatever: ACTION! Tommy walks through the door, gives the transom the stink-eye, shouts, "I did not hit her! I did nahhtt!" and hurls the water bottle. The Grip jumped into the air and yelled! Tommy looked up and said, "Oh, hi Mark!" and walked upstage to Greg. CUT!

Aha! Success! Who says filmmaking isn't fun?!

Mark and Peter Therapy Session: You can imagine my joy at filming a therapy session with Mark and Peter. First, Peter must beg Mark to open up. Well, yeah... after all, Mark is the strong, silent, brooding, angry hero type. First we can't get him to open up; then, we can't get him to shut up. Predictably, Mark wants to kill himself. Suicide in the face of relationship issues is sort of a "Room" tradition.

No! Wait! Mark doesn't want to kill himself anymore. Now, he wants to kill Peter! Man, this is one Hell of a therapy session!

Finally, Mark spills his secret. Yes, Yes, the invasion of Normandy is on June 6th! Oops, sorry, wrong secret. Yes, yes, it's Lisa! Mark's been banging Lisa while Johnny is at work! Oh no! Not Lisa! Johnny is your best friend! What were you thinking?!

Peter is mortified... and, Mark is feeling cathartic and

psychologically healed.

What have we learned here? What can we take away from this little mixture of mayhem and madness? Obviously, Lisa is a sociopath.

Oh, Man! Now THAT'S good melodrama!

CHAPTER 8

THE CREW

I want to be <u>very</u> clear about the crew of "The Room." Most of the crew had little or no experience at this, their chosen profession... yet. They were young, green and filled with the excitement and passion of filmmaking. They were all wonderful, dedicated, hard-working youngsters who were simply trying to get their film careers launched. It was nothing more than a surreal twist of fate that landed them all on "The Room." This is a relatively true statement for any project you become attached to, at any point in your career.

Like all films, television shows, commercials and the like, it is <u>always</u> a group effort. I never could have survived and made this film without dedicated, hardworking people filling out the other departments – camera, art, costume, hair, make-up, sound, grips, electricians and production assistants. All these jobs are critically important to the filmmaking process. Nobody makes a movie by themselves. NOBODY!

A few of these wonderful, hard-working and dedicated people are still working in the industry. They are now veteran, film professionals in their own right. I'm sure they look back at "The Room" with the same blend of mixed feelings that I do. Yes, a few have survived. They are now tough and seasoned cinematic warriors. Very few people survive the first year of their film careers.

Allow me to digress...

I stated earlier that I enjoy teaching. This is an excellent trait for a script supervisor to possess because the only way to learn how to actually be a script supervisor is to be aggressive, obnoxious, persistent, and a genuine pain in the ass until you get an experienced veteran script supervisor to take you under their wing and offer you an internship. I learned how to be a script supervisor from a crusty old veteran named, Bob Gary. Bob's credits include: The Searchers, The Flight of the Phoenix, The Diary of Anne Frank, All about Eve, Whatever Happened to Baby Jane, Friendly Persuasion, and a host of other memorable and famous films. I assure you, there is nobody more aggressive and persistent than me. I'm equally sure my friends would happily back me up on this. I wanted to be trained by the best. Bob was the best.

For a large number of specialist careers in the film industry, an internship is the only way you will ever learn your craft. A film degree, if you ever bother to get one, simply teaches you the basics. I swear if I had a dollar for every first year film graduate who proudly puffs out their chest and states, "I am a film Director," I would be a wealthy man. "No, Dude, you're a PA (production assistant). Get your butt off the set and empty the trash cans or the AD's are going to eat you for lunch. And, don't forget to clean the trash out of Heather's trailer." Maybe someday, that hard working kid will be a film Director... but, not today. Today, he's emptying trash cans, cleaning up trailers and parking cars. And, he better do it with a good attitude and a smile on his face or the last words he's going to hear on the project will be, "You are so fucking fired!"

Many years ago I received a phone call from Zalman King. Zalman was teaching a university film appreciation course when he called, "Sandy, would you come into my class and give that one hour lecture you do on script supervisors? Nobody really knows what the Hell you actually do for a living." That pretty much sums it up...

I arrived at Zalman's classroom after my Central America gig; and, the five weeks in the hospital dealing with the parasite and the ensuing bout of pancreatitis I contracted after shooting in the jungle. There were a lot of things infinitely more dangerous than quicksand in that jungle.

I walked in five minutes after his class started. We exchanged the requisite hugs, pats and 'how the fuck are you's,' and completely ignored the 200 shining, smiling, eager, 'I am a film Director' faces. What? We hadn't seen each other in a while and got caught up. You want to work in film? Get used to being ignored...

Zalman hit me with a small barrage of friendly questions regarding the gig, the locations, the underwater work... all light and easy... and all loud enough for his students to hear us. My answers were equally light and easy – jungle shooting, underwater sets, Belize beaches, Julia Roberts baked cookies – no comments about, quicksand, jungle filth, lack of clean water, parasites, dysentery, poisonous vermin, 130 degree temperatures, 100% humidity, hostile guerrillas, armed guards, insane scheduling, bandits, vampire bats... and, that's when I looked up at his students -- 200 eager, excited faces all thinking the same thing, "That's me! Those are the stories I'm going to tell one day! I am a film Director!" Just like Tommy Wiseau, right? Zalman was smirking and waiting for my reaction.

"Sandy... be nice..."

Script supervising and continuity could wait. I had something infinitely more important to tell Zalman's 200 film Directors. I told them exactly what I've been telling you within these pages... exactly what I told Tommy. I told those kids they were watching two veterans greet each other -- no bitching, no complaining, and no griping about near death experiences -- only the fun, artistic highlights, only the positive aspects of my cinematic adventure! And now, I was going to give them some truth... right between the eyes.

You have to earn these stories! For every fun anecdote I traded with Zalman, I had a hundred horror stories of going without sleep and climbing through shit to get the job done. I've worked on three jungle movies – Belize, the Amazon and Tahiti. Two of these locations gave me dysentery, and one gave me a lethal parasite that almost killed me twice. I filmed for a month in Southern Turkey where the temperature shot to 140 degrees every day and the sand flies that came out at night were big enough to carry away small children. I spent a month struggling to breath at 14,000 feet while shooting in the Andes. Working 70 hour weeks under these conditions requires grit, determination and a high tolerance to pain. Mr. I am Director needs a lesson in grace and humility. Mr. I Am Director would never have survived those projects.

Film careers are not handed out like cotton candy. You have to earn your career! You have to want it bad! I looked out over those smiling faces and told them, "This is the hardest, most difficult thing you can do with your lives! If even three of you are still in this business five years after you graduate, it'll be a miracle!" Their faces were no longer shining and smiling. I looked at Zalman, their esteemed and somewhat famous professor. "Am I wrong?" Zalman clasped his hands behind his back... strolled along the front row of those sad little faces... and said, "Sandy, you're wrong... maybe one will make it."

Yes, it's the hardest thing I know how to do. It's also the most rewarding. When the cameras are rolling and the dialogue is crisp and meaningful, and the actors are giving talented performances... everything falls into place... it's almost like music. My friends, those are the happiest moments of my life.

The great David Lean Directed, back-to-back, "Bridge over the River Kwai," "Dr. Zhivago," and "Lawrence of Arabia." He made these movies before monitors, computers and modern equipment. He used cameras the size of Frigidaires. Hard core! He once said, "There is nothing that gives me greater pleasure than talented acting and good dialogue... conversely, nothing angers me more than untalented acting and bad dialogue." After nearly thirty years of highs and lows in the film business, this is the space I currently occupy. I <u>love</u> good acting!

A word about 1st AD's and why I took over this position:

There is nothing more disastrous to a feature film or a television show than an inexperienced or incompetent 1st AD. The good ones are worth their weight in gold. Absolutely! When I arrived on "The Room," I was told Greg Sestero was my 1st AD... a job he had never done before. Uh-oh...

Allow me to digress further...

Regardless of where you shoot on this planet, the problems are <u>always</u> the same. I was working on a four month project in Turkey that was being Directed by Terry

Cunningham. Our 1st AD was Daniel Carrey. These men have earned these titles! These two gentlemen are extremely talented, patient and focused. They are also good friends of mine and we've shot movies on three continents. Film is war... and we've been in the trenches together.

In Turkey, Terry and I would leave a walkie on channel 1and set it next to the monitors. This is the AD's channel... and you'd better have a damn good reason for being on Channel 1. Terry and I had the walkie so we could communicate with Daniel. Communication is everything! We were shooting near Urgup... the temperature was over 125 degrees and conditions were tough. Inexperienced or incompetent crew in critical positions can make tough conditions even tougher... or impossible. These are the players and this is what we heard.

Cast: Daniel – one of the best 1st AD's I've ever worked with -- calm, focused.

Lucine – 2nd AD -- charming, young, driven, completely inept.

Emel – 2nd 2nd AD -- sweet, repeats everything you say, understands nothing.

Daniel: Lucine? Lucine? Hello? Lucine?

Lucine: Oh... Hello Daniel, how are you?

Daniel: Lucine, bring Mario to the set for blocking.

Lucine: Okay, I bring Mario to the set after he his wired by sound.

Daniel: No, don't wire him. We don't need a wire. It's a close up.

Lucine: What's a close up?

Daniel: Never mind, just bring Mario to the set.

Lucine: Okay, I bring Mario to the set when we are done putting wire on him.

Daniel: No, no, no… forget the wire, just bring him to set.

Lucine: Okay, I bring Mario to set.

Daniel: Right now, okay. No wire…

Lucine: No wire.

Daniel: Bring Mario to set. Now.

Lucine: Okay Daniel.

(five minutes and still no Mario on set)

Daniel: Lucine? Lucine? Hello? (a beat) Walkie check. Walkie check. Can anyone hear me? (a beat) Is anyone on Channel 1? Anyone? Fuck, fuck, fuck! Hello? Lucine? Emel? Anyone? (unintelligible Turkish arguing breaks in) Oh God, no … Please take the Turkish off Channel 1. Lucine? Where the Hell are you?!!

Emel: Hi Daniel. This is Emel. How are you?

Daniel: Oh sweet Jesus… Emel, where is Lucine?

Emel: She is busy.

Daniel: Busy? Busy?!!

Emel: Yes, Daniel, very busy. She is helping Mario.

Daniel: Emel, walk to Lucine and tell her to put her earpiece back in her ear.

(two minutes later)

Emel: Hello Daniel, this is Emel.

Daniel: Yessssss…

Emel: Daniel? Daniel?

Daniel: Go for Daniel.

Emel: Daniel, Lucine says the earpiece hurts her ear. (beat) Hello? Daniel?

Daniel: Emel, please tell her to talk to me on her walkie-talkie.

Lucine: Hello Daniel, how are you?

Daniel: Lucine, where is Mario?

Lucine:	He will be there soon.
Daniel:	Where is he?
Lucine:	We are wiring him for sound.

Channel 1 went dead and I saw Daniel storm off the set. As he passed Terry and me, he pitched his walkie into a trash can and simply kept on walking. Terry and I died laughing. I swear I'm not making this up. This is typical. Terry and I heard this coming out of the walkie next to the monitors while we were preparing to shoot Mario's close up… which eventually happened. The schedule must be completed!

I have been a 1ˢᵗ AD a few times during the course of my career – always on small, non-union projects. I have never enjoyed the position. Sometimes, for the good of the film, you do what you have to do to get the job done and make your schedule. On "The Room" I took the job of 1ˢᵗ AD away from Greg and reluctantly gave it to myself. I didn't really enjoy performing those duties; but, an inexperienced AD can destroy a project. "The Room" was small enough and contained enough that it was easier to direct and be the 1ˢᵗ AD rather than rely on an enthusiastic 1ˢᵗ AD with zero experience. I replaced Greg Sestero as 1ˢᵗ AD on day one of shooting "The Room." Greg was extremely relieved. He's a sweet guy… and much too nice to be the 1ˢᵗ AD of "The Room."

Regardless of what you've heard, "The Room" was a hard gig. Yes, I had a ton of fun; but, I had to work my ass off with a green crew, green actors and Tommy Wiseau. I also had to make script notes for Post Production or the editor never would have been able to cut it together. It was a chaotic three ring circus. It was a cavalcade of errors. An inexperienced Director or 1ˢᵗ AD would have unintentionally killed the project. Nothing would have gotten done in a timely and efficient manner. The editor would have been unable to cut the footage together. Problem solving was the order of the day, on nearly every camera setup and take! "Sandy, the next scene needs to be on a rooftop in San Francisco." Sure, okay, this is what I'll need...

Problem solving requires experience! This means "The Room" was either Directed by someone with my background... or, by a man whose extemporaneous range of creativity for an entire scene was limited to, "Hello Doggy."

But, I digress...

Tommy Wiseau, like all Producers, was in charge of the crew list (and IMDB credits). I have attached the top few inches of the original crew list (below). As you can see, Tommy never quite knew how to deal with me. When you walk around claiming to be Mr. I Am Director, you're bound to have a problem with the guy who really is directing your project. Just because you print it, doesn't make it true.

THE ROOM
CREW LIST
(9/3/02)

PRODUCTION		
Director	Tommy Wiseau	
AD/Script Supervisor/Whatever	Sandy Schklair	818/703-0999 h
	sandyman@socal.rr.com	818/617-7797 p
	sandman@bobsledder.com	

It took Tommy five years to finally get people to notice this film; but, he did get them to notice it. However, like most people who live a faux existence, he knows how to cover his tracks and create an illusion that people have bought into for fourteen years. He knows how to destroy all footage and stills of me as I worked to create this film that has become his entire sad existence.

Yes, most of my crew was young, green and filled with the passion of filmmaking. They are all worthy of acknowledgment in this book if for no other reason than the courage they displayed in choosing to pursue a career in film. How did they arrive on my set? How did they get there? What sin had they committed in a previous life that would deserve a karmic sentence on "The Room?"

The reasons and routes one takes that ultimately land them on a particular film or television crew at a particular date and time during the course of their career, are as varied as all the tourists on all the streets in Los Angeles. For most of the world, unemployment is horrible, dire news, a shock to the system and a fairly good reason to panic... and maybe reach for a pack of razor blades. For those who dare test their mettle in the film industry, unemployment becomes a way of life. Every time your film wraps... you're unemployed. Every time your television show is canceled... you're unemployed. Every time your television show is picked up and you're not 'invited' back... you're unemployed. Every time you hear the immortal words, "You are so fucking fired!" you're unemployed. By the way, not being 'invited' back is simply a polite way of telling you, "Our show got picked up for another season... but, we gave your job to someone else." Maybe the reasons were valid... maybe they weren't. Either way, you're checking the boxes 'no-no-yes-no-no-no,' making phone calls and sending out your resume.

How did these passionate, enthusiastic youngsters arrive on the crew of "The Room?" I have absolutely no idea.

The crew was already in place when I was hired by Tommy. Naturally, this is exactly the opposite of how the system is supposed to work. Doing things the opposite of how they actually get done on "normal" projects was standard operating procedure for "The Room." Let's not forget, I was hired on the same day I started shooting. This never happens! Unless, of course, you have a guy with a mountain of equipment, no experience and a penchant for saying, "I am Director."

Raphael and I were the only veteran film professionals at the start of the project. We never really kept in touch after he drove away after the seventeenth day of shooting. And, the rest of the crew? Life happens... the years pass... friendships fade... and, every now and then, on a new film set, I'll cross paths with someone who worked on "The Room." We trade stories and anecdotes with the crew around us listening... standing there with mouths agape and never quite believing the stories we tell.

Raphael left and was replaced by my friend Graham who shot the remainder of the film. Graham is a good friend and a consummate cinematographer. He's still having trouble owning up to his contribution to "The Room" and I will respect his privacy.

The project really was a comedy of errors. In order to fully appreciate all the errors and not feel overwhelmed, you need experience. Raphael is very experienced and definitely appreciated the comedy cavalcade. Before I explain the extent of Raphael's appreciation, I need to explain a piece of equipment called a "floppy."

Four by Four Floppy: A '4x4' floppy' is a 4' x 8' rectangle of heavy black cloth folded in half and mounted to a 4' square metal frame that can be inserted into a stand

and placed in front of a light to flag off, and shape, the light according to the DP's needs. If the DP needs the full 8' length, you simply tug a couple Velcro closures and unfold the material. This flag can be placed at any angle you choose. There is a reason I explained this. I promise.

As I said, Raphael certainly appreciated the wonderful comedy of errors. So much so, that every time I rolled the camera he would scream with laughter and screw up the sound track. The solution, of course, was to build him a small 4x4 floppy house just outside the stage door. I stuck a chair and a monitor inside and gave him a walkie-talkie. Every time I rolled, he shrieked gleefully at the mistakes. I could still hear him through the stage door, but the volume was low enough to keep his laughter off the sound track. Raphael was a happy man. Every day of shooting brought him closer to getting away from the project... which was really his only goal.

The really insane issue was why Tommy insisted we shoot two fixed mounted cameras – an Arri BL and a Panasonic HD – side-by-side. I practically needed a crane dolly to support the weight. And, going in for close-ups with two fixed mounted cameras was both impossible and hilarious. To this day, neither Graham nor Raphael nor I have any idea why we were using two fixed mounted cameras. The only reason was, "Tommy wants it that way." Sure, why the Hell not. He's paying the bills.

The sound team deserves mention...

The man at the mixing board was a really nice guy and a talented Hungarian musician; but, he wasn't a film sound mixer. He knows recording studio equipment. In fact, he had never mixed sound on a film set before. I'm directing a movie with a sound mixer who had never mixed sound before. Funny, right? He spent the entire first week of the production reading the operating manual for the mixing board. I discovered this fact on our first day of shooting.

Me: "Roll Sound... (nothing) Roll Sound... (nothing) Roll Sound!!"
Mix: "I can't! Wait! Wait! Not yet! Not yet! I'm still reading the manual!"
Me: "Sigh... Take 5 everybody..."

Ultimately, he figured out the mixing board and did a wonderful job.

Predictably, if the sound mixer had never mixed sound before, it stands to reason the boom operator had never held a boom before. I had to cut my shots many times to go onto the set and turn his boom around... because he had the wrong end of the microphone pointed at the actors. It's all part of the process and I never really minded. I did, however, require him to give me a dollar every time his boom hit the wall. I was wearing headphones and he was giving me headaches...

Two other crew deserve mention.

The grips and electricians on "The Room" were always leaving the show for better paying gigs. Usually, they would have somebody show up to replace them... usually. I tried to tune the rotating world of grips and electricians out of my consciousness, as I had more than enough gremlins and demons to deal with. The grips and electricians are led by the best boy grip and best boy electric. "The Room" was small enough that we had one best boy in charge of both departments. Our best boy was Justine Cook and not a boy at all. Justine is tiny, capable and tough as steel... and I had worked with her prior to this project. She provided me a comfort level that cannot be overstated.

The woman shooting the publicity stills on "The Room" was Dina Khouri. Dina is an extremely talented still photographer and studio artist. Her illustrations are featured throughout this book. Tommy Wiseau tends to forget to credit Dina when he reproduces her work. That will not happen in this book and Dina's name certainly belongs on the front cover. Her story is truly amazing. She was born in Beirut. When Dina was thirteen, she and her family were forced to flee their homeland during the Lebanese civil war with nothing more than the clothes on their backs. The Khouri family managed to escape to Cyprus on the last bullet riddled plane to leave Beirut before the airport was shut down. Dina is perhaps the most honest person I have ever met. She walks through life without guile or subterfuge and is loved by everyone who meets her. This makes her unique in Hollywood. Dina has always loved movies… and was determined that she would one day be one of those names in the credits at the end of the films she loved to watch. Dina made her dream happen.

Tommy made his dream happen too. You know what? Tommy's got nuthin' on Dina.

CHAPTER 9

TOMMY'S TWO LOVE SCENES
or
I RESIGN ON THE LAST DAY

I have heard Tommy Wiseau repeat countless versions about how, and why, I left his project. I wonder if even he remembers the truth. I rather doubt it. Allow me to tell the TRUTH about my departure from "The Room," and set the record straight.

On the third day of shooting, during the drunk/pizza eating scene, all Tommy had to do was simply lean over and gently kiss Lisa on the cheek. That's it. Nothing more. A bit of a pucker, a slight turn of the head, a soft brush of lips on Lisa's cheeks, and nobody gets hurt. Easy peasy, right? So simple, a prepubescent teenager could, and would, have given a satisfactory performance. But no, this was never going to be simple.

I was neither fabricating nor embellishing the truth when I said that Take 1 of that 'kiss' was shocking to me and I really did scream, "CUT!" Okay, maybe I didn't wash my eyes out with bleach… but, I sure as Hell wanted to. And yes, I really did tell Tommy/Johnny, "If I ever see your tongue on camera again, I'm going to cut it off!" I wasn't kidding. There are some lines I will not cross and

Tommy's tongue was exceptionally close to the edge of that line.

I believe Tommy's response was something like, "But, Sandy, I have to kiss her."

"Yes, kiss her... not eat her face! Jesus Christ, it's a simple kiss! This is a woman's face, not a bowl of chop suey!" I grabbed Dina and softly kissed her cheek. "Like that! Okay?! For the love of God, Man!"

Tommy finally cooperated and I got a kiss that worked; although, it was not the kiss I wanted... and, Juliette took it like a trooper. I handed Juliette a towel and we continued shooting. The moment was forgotten... by Tommy. I <u>never</u> forgot that moment and I never will. I immediately scheduled his two, nude love scenes for the last day of shooting. I felt his love scenes had the distinct potential to derail the project before it had even really begun. Put on your Director's hat and think about it. I was working with a sensitive young actress. I was absolutely convinced that Tommy's two nude love scenes might cause her to walk off the project. That Day 3 kiss lingered in the back of my mind throughout the remainder of principal photography. I worried and fretted about Tommy's two nude love scenes and constantly worked on formulating some kind of an approach. Nothing came to mind...

There were many occasions during the ensuing weeks that I underscored, "Here in Hollywood, we always save love scenes for the last day of shooting... when the male and female actors are most comfortable with one another." We're talking two full love scenes here! We're talking delicate nuances! We're talking love scenes with Tommy/Johnny and Juliette in intimate and romantic positions! I'm a fairly creative filmmaker; and even with my fertile imagination I knew Tommy's nude love scenes would exceed my sensibilities. I've made my fair share of questionable choices and bad decisions in my life; but, I knew I was standing at the edge of the abyss. I'd just as soon not send my soul plunging into the eternal flames of Hell. I needed a solid approach. I needed rules and boundaries!

Shooting tasteful love scenes for feature films is very difficult. Pornography is easy... aesthetically pleasing PG or R rated love scenes are neither easy nor simple. Love scenes are not the voyeuristic thrill newbies and civilians think they are. You shoot them on a closed set – only those crew members who are absolutely necessary to the shooting process are there. This still adds up to at least six or seven people... hardly an intimate setting. Everybody is uncomfortable to some degree. Add in multiple takes and multiple camera angles and it's positively eerie, "Caress her left breast upstage from the camera please." Seriously, regardless of the project, every crew member on set for a love scene is somewhat ill at ease and doing their best not to show any overt discomfort. At least, that's how the prevailing wind blows on a normal set. "The Room" was not a normal set, and nothing I did was ever going to make it a normal set.

So... I saved Tommy's two love scenes for the last day of shooting. Long before that last day arrived, I knew I was going to have problems with Tommy; which is why I saved these scenes for the last day of shooting. I was eminently prepared to leave this project if I was unable to reconcile Tommy's needs with my own. I take my responsibilities seriously at all times, regardless of how much fun I'm having. I knew if I was forced to resign on the last day, I had still performed my duties to the best of my ability and Directed "The Room" in such a fashion that it actually had a chance to be noticed by fans of the "Late Night Genre." If Tommy forced me to resign, I would only have missed directing his two love scenes. The film could be easily cut together by any competent editor and my conscience would be clear. The second unit footage in San Francisco was never my responsibility. That's why it's called second unit and falls under the responsibility of the second unit Director.

During the previous month's shooting, I had come to know Tommy on many levels. At the most basic level, I can say without hesitation and for the record... Tommy is inordinately proud of his ass! Believe me, this is a massive understatement. I knew, beyond a shadow of a doubt, he would want it featured prominently in his love scenes... and on set... and off set... and in the parking lot... and on La Brea Boulevard. I've spent time around world class body builders and rock-hard super models that are not as overtly proud of their derrieres as Tommy is of his. For four weeks I watched him ask anyone within arm's reach to feel his muscles and touch his ass. The self-proclaimed comparisons to Van Damme were getting tedious to say the least... and I was about to shoot his love scenes. Tommy Wiseau's love scenes... How the fuck did I end up here? What existential sin was I being punished for? My imagination was running rampant. This is not why I left a medical career in Chicago! I would rather have put on a meat-suit and jumped into a pit filled with rabid dogs.

I will NOT direct pornography! This is non-negotiable and a deal breaker. This is absolute. There is no wiggle room here for negotiation. None. Nada. I've made a lot of compromises during the course of my career. Pornography will never be one of my compromises. At the end of the day, I still have to go home, look in the mirror and live with myself. I needed to establish concrete rules and boundaries. I also had a young actress to protect. This was paramount!

After we wrapped camera the night before the last day, I finally had my conversation with Tommy. I confronted him with my rules. My inviolate, set in concrete, rules.

Rule #1: You will <u>not</u> walk around naked on set all day!

TW: But, Sandy, I am European.
Me: I don't give a damn what planet you come from. You will NOT walk around in
 the nude on this set. Non-negotiable!
TW: We'll see…
Me: No. We won't.

Rule #2: You will wear a "sock" (tied around the waist with mono-filament) and <u>only</u> disrobe when the cameras are ready to roll.

TW: But, Sandy, how will I get into character?
Me: You're an actor… pretend you're naked.

Rule #3: You will <u>not</u>, under <u>any</u> circumstances attempt to have sex with Juliette!

TW: But, Sandy, it has to be real!
Me: I Quit! That's it! I am GONE! I resign! I am outta here!
TW: Sandy, you can't quit.
Me: Watch me!

And that was that. I had performed my directing duties to the best of my abilities and the film could be easily cut together. My conscience was clear. In filmmaking terms, my producer and I had irreconcilable differences and we had arrived at an artistic impasse. I was free to resign.

I told Tommy I would be happy to make some phone calls and try and find him a Director for his two love scenes. He absolutely refused. He insisted that Greg Sestero, his assistant, a man who had <u>never</u> Directed, would direct his love scenes with Juliette.

In retrospect, given the perverted nature of Denny wanting to "watch," and being informed by my crew that Tommy spent the entire day walking around naked on set, I clearly made the correct decision. He had Denny say, "I want to watch..." Are you fucking kidding me?! This is beyond inappropriate -- boundaries, Tommy, boundaries! Had I been on set that last day, I would have put an end to that sick bullshit instantly. It's bad enough that he had his editor start the film with his bare ass close up. His naked ass... Denny wants to watch... What the Hell was he thinking?!

Talk about gratuitous egocentricity. Tommy's two love scenes primarily consisted of his naked ass bobbing up and down in camera; and, hearing him moaning and groaning with Lisa buried underneath him.

I did not direct these two scenes! Please do not blame me for them! They are not my fault! Like many other aspects of "The Room," I was merely a victim of circumstances. (I finally get to quote Curly Howard. Big moment!)

And so, I resigned... and, while my "Room" crew was shooting Tommy's two love scenes on that fateful last day, I began working on another project. I was fortunate to be asked to work as script supervisor on "Jumbo Girl," a short film being shot by Janusz Kaminsky. Let's weigh my decision here shall we... On the one hand I could spend my day fighting with Tommy and staring at his naked ass for twelve hours… or, on the other hand, I could work with Janusz Kaminsky, a cinematographer with two Oscars on his shelf. No contest! No hesitation!

Tommy Wiseau didn't quite see things my way. What a shock! Tommy took my name off the film as Director and excluded me from the editing process. Tommy has also spent the past fourteen years bashing me on the internet and in the press. He has never returned my phone calls or emails and denies their existence to the media. It would appear I bruised his delicate and fragile feelings when I left the project. When Tommy invited Dina Khouri to the wrap party, he told her, "Sandy can't come to the wrap party. He quit. I don't like him anymore." I assure you, the feeling is mutual.

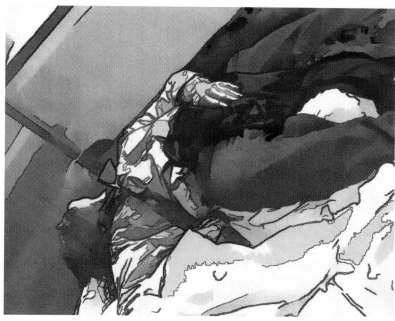

CHAPTER 10

THE MEDIA REACTS

Yes, I Directed "The Room." And, I left on the last day of shooting…

And, Tommy put his face on a billboard above Highland Avenue for the next five years; which was a fairly shrewd move.

I promised to tell the truth in my book and this is obviously the proof. It is extremely difficult for me to use the word "Tommy" and "shrewd" in the same sentence. Still, it was a clever, albeit expensive, marketing ploy and the curiosity of the viewing public was piqued. It worked for Angelyne. It worked for Daisy Clover. Why wouldn't it work for Tommy?

Given the materials I had to work with and the arena I stepped into, absurdity was the only goal I could aim for. I had a million dollars' worth of equipment, no full script, an inexperienced cast and crew, three pages of daily weirdness and a small sound stage. Everything about the movie is atrocious and outrageous. Absurdity was the goal! My job, as I saw it, was to steer the wreckage into an entertaining place and make sure nobody got hurt. My approach worked beyond my wildest imagination...

Newspapers and magazines slowly started noticing the rise of this cult film. Sure, "Rocky Horror" and "Big Trouble in Little China" are wonderful, "good" little cult films, each beloved for their own uniqueness. Certainly, the acting and the scripts were far superior to "The Room" in every regard. So what? "The Room" was being noticed for its over-the-top absurdity. Yes, it's a horrible, terrible, abominable little film that goes miles over the top. That's the appeal. Never in my wildest imagination could I have foreseen how audiences would react! Yelling ribald comments! Reciting the dialogue along with the characters! And, my absolute favorite; throwing plastic spoons at the screen! I LOVE THAT!
The spoons started as a stupid joke with the camera operator, and it has remained a stupid joke for 14 years. There are fans that have literally seen this movie fifty times or more. It's simple, stupid fun!

And, that's pretty much the way I Directed it – simple, stupid fun.

Tommy Wiseau was the only person who didn't, or couldn't, see the comedic aspects of the weirdness that was "The Room." I swear it wasn't just me! There was a lot of laughter on that set. Except with Tommy – always the serious Marlon Brando wannabe filled with angst...

and a tunnel vision focused on the soul of Stanley Kowalski. Marlon Brando's talent was, of course, completely absent. The crew was usually giggling uncontrollably mixed with bouts of apoplectic fits of laughter! So that's what I used. Infuse Tommy with as much Stanley Kowalski as I could and set him loose on the other actors. Honestly, you have to go for a lot of takes before you get a properly absurd version of, "You are tearing me apart, Lisa!" Guess what? It worked!

Film critics tend to take the craft a bit seriously and many have trouble sinking low enough to find the appeal that millions of fans seem to have found with this movie. That's fine with me. "The Room" is an acquired taste and certainly not for everyone.

There are a vast number of celebrities who have watched and loved, "The Room." A short list would include Rob Lowe, Paul Rudd, Jonah Hill, David Cross, and Edgar Wright, the Director of "Shaun of the Dead." Kristen Bell hosts "Room" parties at her house. The list of camp loving celebrities is nearly endless. They "get it." I was working with Rob Lowe on "Franklin & Bash." Malcolm McDowell told him I was the guy who actually Directed the movie… Rob Lowe cornered me in my Director's chair with a very intense look on his face, "You?! You're the guy who really Directed that movie?! I LOVE THAT MOVIE!" Thank you, Rob.

This is part of the problem. Half the professionals in Hollywood know I Directed this movie; at least, those professionals who have actually heard of "The Room." Sadly, in this business, it's infinitely more fun to keep the controversy alive and never actually print the truth. I haven't really minded until now. You know… let sleeping dogs lie. Unfortunately, this dog won't lie down. This dog is completely out of control. This dog never, ever goes away! "Hi Doggy!"

A Professor of film studies at the State University of Minnesota called "The Room," "One of the most important films of the past decade. It exposes the fabricated nature of Hollywood." No shit. This is why it's called, Tinsel Town. Still, if educated – and possibly deranged -- cinephiles want to refer to "The Room" as one of the most important films of the past decade; then they're probably in desperate need of therapy. On the other hand, perhaps it wouldn't be so terrible if my name were rightfully and truthfully attached to it. As you might imagine, being the Director of the "worst film ever made" is a very keen, double edged sword.

In December of 2008, Clark Collis, a writer and editor for Entertainment Weekly magazine, interviewed Tommy Wiseau as the Director of "The Room." I read the interview with incredulity! Tommy insisted he always intended the movie be partly comedic. This is bullshit. This is a lie! Tommy took credit for the absurd humor I put into the movie; primarily because this is what the fans loved. Aha! Now he gets it! It only took 10 years for him to get the joke; better late than never, right? I know I'm beating a dead horse here... perhaps an entire herd of dead horses... but, Tommy never, ever, thought "The Room" was a comedy until millions of fans were laughing their collective asses off. This is exactly why I'm writing this book. I've been swimming in the Hollywood shark pond for a very long time. Liars are part of the scenery here. Liars are a fact of life. Still, it's irritating; and, it's personal. The man told lies about me. And now, I'm a character in a major motion picture; and the filmmakers have never bothered to talk to me. Can you imagine? What if it was you?

Clark Collis interviewed a lot people for that 2008 article. He never interviewed me. I wore three hats on "The Room" and I wasn't interviewed for the article. I don't blame Clark. I'm sure he didn't even know I existed. Tommy Wiseau made sure of that. I Directed Tommy's movie and saved his ass. This is the truth he desperately needs to hide.

Remember "Singing in the Rain?" Debbie Reynolds is the on-screen voice of the nasty and nasal-sounding lead actress, Lina Lamont (Jean Hagen), who will do anything to keep the truth hidden. That's me, the Debbie Reynolds of, "The Room." (I am going to take a mountain of crap for that sentence.) Naturally, Tommy wishes I would contract a fatal illness; or, perhaps move into a yurt in Outer Mongolia and raise shaggy sheep. Regardless, I am now, and always have been, the one man Tommy Wiseau needs to keep buried as best he can. Frankly, I'm surprised he never tried to pay me for my silence. That's certainly his style. Be that as it may, Clark never interviewed me for the 2008 article and Tommy was allowed to continue pretending he Directed "The Room."

Predictably, I continued to rant to my friends whenever I read about him in print or heard him in an interview. I was on the set of "Franklin & Bash" and ranting about some irritating sentence of Tommy's that started with the words, "A real Director knows…" I never made it to the end of the sentence. I got pissed off. I ranted and annoyed everyone around me, including Malcolm McDowell. In an effort to stop my annoying rants, Malcolm outed me to Entertainment Weekly.

Clark Collis interviewed me shortly thereafter and in February of 2011 he wrote an article titled: "The Battle over the Worst Movie Ever Made." In the previous chapters, I have explained and answered all the vagaries and questions this article raises. You now possess the truth about "The Room."

Please, put on your empathy hats and read this article from my perspective.

> *Why would anyone demand a Director's credit on a notoriously awful film? Welcome to the latest chapter in the insane saga of "The Room."*

> *Many Directors have fought to get their names removed from bad films. Sandy Schklair might be the first person in Hollywood history who wants credit for making one. And not just any bad movie. The veteran script supervisor is asking for recognition for directing what many regard as the worst film of all time: 2003's The Room. "That movie is mentioned by crew people constantly here in Los Angeles," says Schklair, 53. "It's very difficult not to say, 'Excuse me, I Directed that!"*

> *The credited Director of The Room is Tommy Wiseau, a mysterious gentleman of unknown age and origin who was also the movie's writer, producer, distributor, and star. Wiseau released his debut film in June, 2003 in a handful of L.A. cinemas, and it attracted little interest. But not long after the movie's brief theatrical run, Wiseau started to put on midnight shows. Since then, this sex-filled indie drama has become a Rocky Horror-style phenomenon, with*

audiences shouting wisecracks at the screen and hurling plastic cutlery whenever a framed photograph of a spoon appears. The R-rated movie is available on DVD, and YouTube is filled with campy fan homages. The Room's more famous devotees include Paul Rudd, Kristen Bell, David Cross, and Jonah Hill. In his 2009 stand-up DV, My Weakness Is Strong, Patton Oswalt lampooned the Euro-accented Wiseau during a sketch with Jon Hamm. In April of last year, the film screened at New York City's 1,163 capacity Ziegfeld Theater to a sold-out crowd that included Justin Long. And in September, Rob Lowe tweeted that his followers should check out the movie. "I love the writing," Lowe tells EW. "There are scenes that look like you wrote lines of dialogue on a piece of paper, cut them into strips, put them in a hat, shook the hat, arranged them top to bottom, photocopied them, gave them to actors, and told them to act it."

Wiseau maintains that the film's faults – from risible dialogue to over-the-top acting – were intentional choices and that he chose them, not Schklair.

[HE CHOSE?! Tommy can't tell the difference between a comedic choice and a bite on the fanny! Fourteen solid years of this bullshit...]

"I will never give this guy credit," says Wiseau. "He did not direct the movie." Schklair insists that he did — and that Wiseau has "been lying for eight years." And why would Schklair even want credit for creating what he describes as "an abomination"?

[Why? Because I turned this movie into a really <u>funny</u> abomination, that's why! I had a ton of fun doing it! It was rare treat working with Tommy/Johnny/Stanley Kowalski/ Mr. I Am Director! The man was acting in "Gone with the Wind" while I was directing the "The Bellboy!"]

Schklair first met Wiseau in the summer of 2002, at a film-equipment company in North Hollywood. Schklair claims Wiseau asked him not only to work as the movie's script supervisor, but also "to tell the actors what to do, and yell 'Action!' and 'Cut!' and tell the cameraman what shots to get." According to Schklair, their conversation proceeded as follows:

Schklair: Um... you want me to direct your project?
Wiseau: No! I am Director!
Schklair: Yeah, you're the Director; whatever. You want me to direct your movie for you?
Wiseau: Yes, please.

For his part, Wiseau denies hiring Schklair to direct The Room. "He was hired as a script supervisor," he says. "If he was my assistant, so be it. But direct? I don't think so."

[ASSISTANT?! In what universe?! And <u>this</u> from a man who strolls into Hollywood and buys – not rents, mind you – but <u>buys</u> a million dollars' worth of film equipment with no clue how to use it! Greg Sestero was Tommy's assistant. It was his job. He got paid for it. I was paid to direct his damn movie!]

Before The Room, the Chicago born Schklair spent 15 years working as a script supervisor on everything from the TV series Chicago Hope to the 1998 horror movie The Dentist 2. But nothing prepared him for the chaos that awaited him on The Room. Much of the cast and crew lacked serious movie-making experience, and Wiseau insisted on shooting with two cameras – one 35mm, one high-def – mounted side by side, a decision Schklair describes as "insane." Then there was the script. "When the pages first came off Tommy's typewriter, they were nearly unintelligible," Schklair claims. "The actors would descend on me as if I was a quarterback kneeling in a football huddle, fighting for our lives late in the fourth quarter. Then they would begin chanting their mantra; "Please, Sandy, for the love of

God, rewrite this so it makes sense!"
Schklair maintains he was the one who gave the project its comedically berserk vibe. "Tommy never, ever, ever, ever saw the humor that we were throwing into it," he says. "I would go home and scream with laughter, because he just did not know what was happening at all." At least one Room cast member backs up his version of events. "The script supervisor ended up sort of directing the movie," says the actor, who requested anonymity, "Tommy was so busy being an actor that this other guy Directed the whole thing."

[Someone finally tells the truth... anonymously. Still, it was nice to hear one involved voice tell the truth.]

Wiseau is somewhat vague about whether he was always the person calling "Action!" and "Cut!" but argues there is more to the job of directing than just barking orders: "If I put you on the set right now and I said to you [say] 'Cut' and 'Go' and you expect me to give you credit as a Director? Are you kidding me? That's laughable, my friend!" Wiseau also points out that Schklair left the project before the end of principal photography: "He quit. That's a big, big, big deal."

["Cut" and "Go?" Seriously? The words are "Cut" and "Action." Mr. I Am Director...]

Schklair admits that after working on the movie for more than a month, he resigned the day before Wiseau filmed his love scenes with Juliette Danielle. "Tommy is – what are the right words? – proud of his buttocks," says Schklair. "I had been offered a position working as a script supervisor with [Steven Spielberg's Director of photography] Janusz Kaminski. I could spend my day shooting Tommy's naked ass, or go work with a DP with two Oscars."

[Oh, Hell yes, I quit! It was the LAST day of principal photography. I had done my job to the best of my ability. His damn love scenes would just have to happen without me! I mercifully spared myself that indelible bit of brain trauma!]

At the time, Schklair's lack of a directing credit didn't seem like a huge deal. "Nobody was ever going to see this anyway," he says. But three years ago, after returning from the Bulgarian set of the 2009 Morgan Freeman, Antonio Banderas vehicle The Code, he discovered The Room had become a cult sensation. "I came back from Europe and it was everywhere, I could not believe it. Who could?" Schklair claims he left messages for Wiseau asking to discuss the credit situation but never received a response. "I have tried to contact Tommy, saying, 'I would like my name on this as Director,'" he explains.

"I have never had one phone call or email returned. And frankly, that pisses me off." Wiseau denies being contacted by Schklair.

[Fortunately, I've kept copies of every email I ever sent Tommy.]

Last fall, Schklair was hired as the script supervisor for TNT's new legal dramedy Franklin & Bash. It was there that he got the idea to go public – from none other than cast regular Malcolm McDowell. "Malcolm says, 'Why haven't you gone to the press?'" Schklair recalls. "He goes, 'You're pissed off? Go tell your story."

So, what now? Schklair has ambitions to direct – or is that direct again? – and thinks he'll have a better shot if people are aware of his role in crafting The Room. "If this should catch Roger Corman's eye and he goes, 'Yeah, I could put this guy through the wringer,' I would love that," he says. The chances of that happening are not so ludicrous; given The Room's ever growing cult and Wiseau's plan to re-release it theatrically in – yes – 3-D. "We want to do it because I'm obsessed about 3-D right now, if you ask me, says Wiseau. Even if Schklair doesn't advance up Hollywood's greasy pole, he says he has no regrets about his involvement in the Citizen Kane of bad films. "Yes, we were making

*the world's worst movie," he says. "But,
we knew it at the time. I embraced The
Room. What a blast!"*

That Entertainment Weekly article was written in 2011.
Nobody really cared about the truth of "The Room" in
2011. My career as a script supervisor was, and is, going
along well. I once again took the 'high road' and let the
lies, slurs and insults slide. But, with the release of the
Franco/Rogen film "The Disaster Artist" along with the
pending release of the documentary "Room Full of
Spoons" and, a resurgent interest in "The Room," I think
it's time I now set the record straight. I have no choice. I
am tired of reading lies about me. Is this so hard to
understand?

This is Hollywood, if I don't tell the truth, who the Hell
will? Tommy? No. He wishes I were in a Russian gulag
north of the Arctic Circle. James Franco and Seth Rogen?
No. As honored as I am that Seth is playing me in their
feature, which will be released world-wide, neither he nor
James nor their screenwriter has ever wanted to talk to
me. Bewildering, no? Is the truth (and my dignity) going
to be, once again, sacrificed for laughs and box office
success?

Did Greg Sestero and Tom Bissell tell the truth? Sort of...
Their book does kind of treat me fairly, but doesn't
actually tell the truth now, does it? There's an awful lot
missing. On the other hand, Greg is a good guy and I
consider him a friend. I'm sure Tommy brought all sorts
of unpleasant pressure on him when the book was being
written.

I was going to discuss Yvonne Villarreal's front page Los
Angeles Times article about "The Room" (October,

2009); but Yvonne simply wrote the same crap everyone else wrote about the room, so there's really no point beating that herd of horses again.

I liked the IMDB review that said, "This film is like getting stabbed in the head." I thought that was pretty funny. Frankly, and in all honesty, this is <u>exactly</u> what I was going for. Welcome to my world, Room fans! I was getting stabbed in the head, twelve hours a day, for an entire month. Personally, I thought the bizarre essence of "The Room" was hilarious and Tommy Wiseau's presence on film is as hypnotic as a 10 car fatal crack-up on the freeway. You just <u>have to</u> look! Mission accomplished!

CHAPTER 11

THE INTERNET

Okay... the internet. I'll admit, I don't really pay attention to the "The Room" fan base. In point of fact, I intentionally avoid it. I'm sure you can understand why. I simply <u>cannot</u> believe the amount of "Room" material on the internet! It's unbelievable! Don't you people have jobs?

Again, I feel compelled to write the words, "Worst movie ever made?!" It may be the strangest, stupidest, oddest, weirdest, funniest, most bizarre movie ever made; but worst? I'm sorry, but the worst movie ever made doesn't generate this magnitude of interest. Any film made in Hollywood that generates this level of interest is considered a success! Use any measuring stick you want. Love it or hate it, this movie succeeded in getting noticed and building a fan base. Fourteen years later, the popularity of "The Room" continues to grow. This is the definition of "Success" in Hollywood. This is not open to debate. This is fact.

I simply cannot comment on all the countless websites and uploads regarding "The Room." I would be writing for the next ten years. I decided to watch a small collection of the tastiest internet submissions and make a few appropriate comments. I chose sites that reviewed and passed judgment on the movie and avoided sites that featured interviews with Tommy, Greg or any of the other cast members. It's very difficult for me to watch Tommy Wiseau giving an interview. It would seem I have issues...

EVERYTHING WRONG WITH "THE ROOM" IN 8 MINUTES OR LESS:

Okay, this is my favorite so I'll start with this one. This guy rattles off so many criticisms it's ridiculous; and, he does it in 8 minutes. I can't comment on everything; but, I'll pick a few of my favorites…

First, I will make the same statement I always make about "Room" critiques. 1) Do NOT take this movie seriously! Ever! The movie is, was, and always will be, absurd, surreal and bizarre. 2) I didn't write the dialogue… I survived the dialogue. However, I freely admit that I loved the horrible words. They are just so, so bad. So bad, it almost hurts to listen. This is scripted dialogue you will never find anywhere else in the entire gamut of film and television. It's just so completely, bloody awful. I've worked on countless projects with good dialogue… but, "The Room" is the only movie I've ever worked on where the dialogue was so terrible it was hypnotic. The worse it became, the more I enjoyed it! I've spent my entire career meticulously guarding and crafting lines for actors. I've never had the freedom to be so irreverent… I suppose, in a sense, directing "The Room" was both cathartic and therapeutic for me.

Tommy wrote the script… and, as a professional filmmaker, I was endlessly fascinated by the fact that he couldn't start a single scene or conversation without the characters saying "hi" to each other. I would have pointed this out to Tommy and suggest he stop doing it; but, I couldn't… I was laughing too hard.

And, for the record, I agree with every comment here.

126

These horrible flaws are part of the reason why this movie is loved by so many millions of fans. I love the flaws. The flaws add personality to this film. I added almost as many flaws to this movie as Tommy did. Come on, be honest... If you were directing this movie, you would have done the same thing. It was irresistible... "Tommy, be sure to say 'Hi' to the other characters in the scene." Don't hate me, laugh with me...

My Favorite Remarks on this video:

- *Tommy's dialogue coach was Nick Riviera.*
- *Pillow fighting is foreplay, and Denny is a creepy bastard.*
- *Tommy reads lines he wrote like he doesn't understand them.*
- *"If you love me you'll drink this." This is how the Jonestown Massacre started.*

Okay, it just goes on and on like this; but, like most sites that critique "The Room," it's the viewer comments that I like the most.

- *Tommy is resurrected as a cyborg and sent back in time to kill Mark and Lisa.*
- *This should have been called, "Everything is wrong with 'The Room'" and then just played the movie.*
- *There's so much awkward sex in this movie it feels like it was written by a 20 year old virgin.*
- *I am a 20 year old virgin and I could write a better sex scene.* [Awesome!]
- *Even "Twilight" is better than this shit!* [No it isn't...]

- *After years of watching hilarious reviews of this movie, I still don't know what the plot is...* [Neither do I, dude, neither do I...]
- *This is my favorite movie!* [Thank you, Jonathan... and, please see a therapist]

What I love most about this video is how fast the reviewer tags everything wrong with the movie. He even counted all the "Hi's" and how many times the football is tossed. This is priceless! He hit on almost everything. Almost... There are still a few things you guys don't know.

FANBOY FLICKS:

This is a video people throw at me a lot. The gentleman on Fanboy Flicks states that "The Room" gets more requests for review by him than any other film. Really?! I don't quite know what to say to that. You should only review a movie that takes itself seriously. "The Room" should not be reviewed... it should be experienced!

According to Fanboy, this is an easy movie to break apart. I agree. He's right. This movie can be summarized in 3 or 4 sentences. Of course, as a film professional, I would like to point out that ALL movies can be summarized in 3 or 4 sentences. These are the 3 or 4 sentences you use at Network and Studio pitch meetings. Although, when Entertainment Weekly asked me what the movie was about, I replied honestly, "I really don't know... Yes, I Directed the movie... and, I'm telling you straight up, I really don't know what the Hell this movie is about." It's been 14 years and I still don't know...

Fanboy starts his review by repeating something Tommy has said many times. The script for "The Room" was going to be a play... and then he was going to turn it into a 500 page novel. Sure. Why not? "The Room" will fit neatly with other great 500 page novels, such as <u>War and Peace</u> and <u>Les Miserables</u>. Can you imagine expanding "The Room" into a 500 page novel? You could make it required reading in high security prisons. I can't imagine a greater deterrent to crime than being forced to read a 500 page "Room" novel. Waterboarding would be kinder...

I love that Fanboy showed a clip of Lisa sweeping the

floor. My friends… This was the funniest scene I shot in the entire movie! I swear, from the bottom of my bottom. Lisa sweeping the floor is the only portion of this scene that made it into the final cut. I had the rest of the film destroyed. What made it so funny? I'm not going to tell you! This will have to remain a mystery. Sorry. Perhaps if you run into me at a party and ply me with drinks…

Fanboy claims Tommy stated the movie was made for $6 Million. He's amazed and astonished. Frankly, so am I. This movie did not cost $6 Million. You'll have to trust me on this. I've worked on countless feature films and TV shows. I know how and where money is spent when shooting. Tommy did not spend $6 Million producing this delicious monstrosity. Fanboy mentions that Tommy said the money was used to replace a lot of the cast and crew… Say what?! Any professional film accountant will tell you, whether you replace cast and crew or not, the budget stays the same. Exhausting, no?

Fanboy goes on about the opening love scene and how Denny wants to participate. Every critic slams the love scenes. I slammed the love scenes. I already talked about the inappropriate nature of Denny's character. Denny is like the Danny Boniduce of "The Room." His dialogue always made me wince and worry about spending eternity in Hell. Fortunately, the football kept his hands busy.

As I explained, Tommy's love scenes were shot on the day I resigned. I resigned because of his two nude love scenes. Had I been there, I would have cut these love scenes down to a couple of minutes. I would have taught Tommy where vaginas are normally located on human females… As Fanboy points out, it doesn't appear that Tommy understands that vaginas grow south of a woman's belly button.

He also points out that Mom gives terrible advice. No shit. As a mother, she fits somewhere between Joan Crawford and Lucretia Borgia.

Fanboy then seems to get caught up in the pointless nature of the scenes. Of course the scenes are pointless. The entire film is pointless... and, that's the point! Why doesn't he understand this?

The only real problem I have with Fanboy's review is the fact that he, like so many others, is trying to take this film somewhat seriously. This is a mistake! You are not supposed to take this film seriously. Reviewing "The Room" from a serious point of view is like trying to critique "The Three Stooges" from a serious point of view. Would you critique Moe for inaccurate eye poking? Would you critique Curly for not really being a victim of circumstances? How about analyzing the accuracy of whether or not you can really pull out huge clumps of Larry's hair... "The Room" is a Three Stooges movie minus the Three Stooges.

My Favorite Viewer Comments:

- *"The Room" is a horror movie with the horror scenes edited out.*
- *Tommy is obviously in his 50s.* [No shit...]
- *When you're so lonely, you fuck a dress.* [I love this comment!]
- *The football is the best actor in the movie.*
- *Only "The Room" can make sex boring.*

NOSTALGIA CRITIC, THE ROOM REVIEW:

Okay... This video was a bit more annoying than most; but, I blame the subject matter more than I blame the critic. The most annoying part was the references to Tommy Wiseau as the Director. However, I liked that he called it the "Best Worst Movie" ever made. I agree with this. Given the circumstances, I was actually doing my best to create the Best Worst Movie ever made. What else could I possibly do?

After you make it through the Nostalgia Critic's opening shtick you arrive at his review of "The Room." At first, he seems stunned that Tommy Wiseau is the lead actor. I was stunned that Tommy was my lead actor too. Although, honestly, Tommy's "stunning" performance is one of the reasons this film is so popular. His lack of talent is shocking... stunning... absolutely horrendous... and, essential to the success of "The Room." Yes, essential. I Directed this movie; but, without Tommy and his persona, there is no movie...

The success of "The Room" is due to three distinct elements; my directing skills, and Tommy's writing and acting "skills." There are moments I truly despise Tommy for the shabby way he's treated me during the past fourteen years. However, I would be foolish not to recognize that his bizarre persona and even more bizarre screenwriting skills contributed greatly to the success of "The Room."

Yes, "The Room" is a successful motion picture. This success is not measured in money. Honestly, I really have no idea how much money "The Room" earned at the box office. No, the success of "The Room" is measured in its millions of fans, millions of critics and the fact that people watch this movie over and over and over... much the same way "Rocky Horror" is deemed a success. "Rocky Horror" certainly had more money, better actors, a better script, and musical numbers. I've often wondered how much better "The Room" would have been with some really horrible, discordant musical numbers. I could easily write the lyrics to "You Are Tearing Me Apart, Lisa." I'm sure you could too.

The Nostalgia Critic also seems a bit weirded out that Denny wants to join Johnny and Lisa in bed for a "nap." Welcome to the club, dude. Nobody was more stunned and shocked by Denny's character than I was. Still, when you're hired to direct a project, you do your best to direct the scenes and characters as the writer and producer intend; such is the nature of directing. However, I toned down the inappropriateness as best I could. You may all thank me for preventing Johnny, Denny and Lisa from having a threesome. I put my foot down on this before it ever came up... because I could actually see this coming up.

I loved when this guy critiqued the love scenes. He had the same reaction as all the other critics of this movie; he just did it better. He attacked the same issues as everyone else. The love scenes were too long... they featured Tommy's naked ass... and Tommy looks like he jammed his penis into Juliette's belly button.

NOTE: The look of disbelief the Nostalgia Critic wears on his face while he reviewed "The Room" is very similar to the look I wore on my face during the entire month I shot the movie. I think of this look as "numbing disbelief." It's the same look you would wear on your face if you walked into the bathroom and saw your grandparents naked.

The rest of the Nostalgia Critic's critique of "The Room" is similar to everyone else's. However, he really does do it better... and he does it for 28 minutes. This is my biggest objection to this site. He critiqued my 99 minute movie for 28 minutes. His critique lasts longer than Tommy's love scenes. How is that even possible? How can you critique this movie for 28 minutes? How?

My Favorite Viewer Comments:

- *I heard this movie was terrible. But my God! "Terrible" is the understatement of the freaking century!*
- *Are all of Johnny's lines dubbed? All his lip movements barely match up.*
  [This is the way he talks, Dude. Tommy's mouth is out of sync with his words. Talking to Tommy is like talking to a character in a poorly dubbed foreign film.]
- *For fuck's sakes this movie is golden shit!* [That's right!]
- *It's entertaining; and, it's re-watchable!* [Damn right it is!]

ENTERTAINMENT WEEKLY ARTICLE – VIEWER COMMENTS:

In the previous chapter, I gave you my comments on the 2011 Entertainment Weekly article written by Clark Collis. I went online and found reader comments on the same article.

Here are a few reader comments and my responses:

- *Sandy did not direct "The Room." It's not true. It's bullshit. He did not direct it. He did NAAAHHHT!*

Well, if you've read the rest of this book, than you realize this person is full of shit. I did indeed direct this movie, and you shouldn't make declarative statements about things you know nothing about! I'm sorry to be the one to shatter your fantasies...

- *Sandy you are no good. You are chicken. Cheep, cheep, cheep, cheep.*

Who knew Tommy would submit his own comments about this article?

The following comment is the sort of comment that has really pissed me off over the years. It's a comment written by a stupid asshole, wannabe who knows nothing and has done nothing. This was also probably written by Tommy. It sure sounds like him.

- *The guy quit and he is not entitled to any credit. And no one in Hollywood should give him any work, he is just a chicken. Why he bean waiting for over 10 years to get a credit. He said that he embraced The Room; well body you should be sorry for your stupid comments and you should apologize to Wiseau who is only Director of The Room.*

I have left the grammar and spelling of this comment exactly the way I found it. According to this insightful genius, I shouldn't get credit for directing this film because I left on the last day. I should also fail in life and die of starvation because I had the temerity to tell the truth. This idiot is a marketing professional's wet dream. A guy like this will believe anything... This jerk is passing judgment on my life! He can't write, he can't spell, he can't formulate intelligent sentences... and then he slams me because he desperately wants to believe someone with Tommy Wiseau's mental acuity can actually direct a movie. The only thing this guy accomplished was to embarrass himself online.

- *I love Sandy. When I grow up, I want to marry him and have his babies.*

Finally! An intelligent and insightful comment!

THE MORNING SHOW: INSIDE THE ROOM:

This is an actual interview with Tommy and Greg. This was extremely painful for me to watch...

There are many sites on the internet and YouTube that have interviews with Tommy. Friends... I just can't watch these anymore. I just can't do it. Tommy sits in front of the cameras and does nothing but spew lies... with sunglasses on. Greg sits next to him, smiling uncomfortably, and you can actually hear the conversation going on in his head as Tommy pontificates. It's positively embarrassing.

When I first saw this interview, and heard Tommy discussing his desire for an Oscar, I nearly threw my coffee mug through my new television set.

This chapter was going to include my pithy and insightful comments on a handful of Tommy Wiseau interviews. But... I just can't do it. I just can't look at him spewing his garbage and then make funny, snarky comments. I just can't look at that face any more than I have to...

I'll tell you what. Someday, when I stand before you giving a lecture about filmmaking or an interview about "The Room," I'll be happy to answer any questions you have and make as many snarky comments as you can handle. I promise.

Let's just put a stake through the internet and move on to my last chapter...

CHAPTER 12

THE FINAL WORD

Yes, I Directed "The Room."

Such a simple statement... and yet, so massive in its scope. Believe me; these words frequently stick in my throat; like swallowing a plastic spoon sideways. Yet, here I am, saying these words out loud; writing them in a book for the world to read. Why? Because, it's the plain and simple truth, that's why. There are plenty of people who know this simple truth – the original crew and cast, my friends, their friends; and, for all I know, your friends as well. The film community is not as large as you might think it is. No matter what project I've worked on during the course of my career, or where it shoots, there are always one or two crew members who know the reality of "The Room" and gleefully share this historical little nugget with the rest of the crew. The amount of good-natured crap I've taken on film sets all over the world is simply not to be believed.

I had a lot of fun directing this movie. Sadly, "The Room" stopped being fun for me long after the project was finished. What a pity.

Let's get deep. "Why are we here? What is the purpose of life?" My answer to this eons old question is, to live an interesting and fulfilling life. I'd like to think I've lived an interesting, fulfilling and amazing life... I've accomplished a great many personal goals; and, I've surmounted challenging hurdles. My reward?! "The Room" is going to be my legacy. For fuck's sake... This is what I'll probably be remembered for. God certainly has a wicked sense of humor. Just look what he did with the duckbill platypus. This gives me comfort.

I dislike liars under most circumstances. The traffic cop in your rear view mirror and the IRS are reasonable exceptions. The film business collects all sorts of souls; from intensely honorable and ethical artists on one end of the bell curve to despicable liars and back-stabbers on the other end of the curve. In the world of filmmaking, both talent <u>and</u> shit float to the top. Our world is neither black nor white; and professional filmmakers mostly tend to inhabit the gray areas of the bell curve. The trick, of course, is to discern the worth and trustworthiness of the people who surround you on the projects that comprise your career. I've met some incredible people on the projects I've worked on. The ability to judge and ascertain a person's character is honed with life experience. This is also a plain and simple truth. Tommy Wiseau produced... he wrote... he acted... and, it would seem, he needs the world to believe he Directed as well.

Ask yourself a simple question, if I wasn't directing this project – and acting as 1st AD and script supervisor -- why would Tommy Wiseau be so upset if I quit?! If I was some assistant of his or only the script supervisor, Tommy wouldn't have given a damn whether I stayed or left.

Crew members were constantly leaving for other gigs. He was angry because I was carrying his entire project for him! Tommy wanted pornography and I didn't. We hit an impasse and I quit. As Director, I designed and blocked every scene, gave <u>all</u> the actors their performance instructions; and controlled the shooting process. As 1st AD, I ran the set and kept things running smoothly off set. I was constantly prepping for the "next" shot. As script supervisor, I was communicating <u>everything</u> relevant that happened on set for Post Production and the editors. I made this film for Tommy Wiseau, my producer. Tommy the producer paid my salary and gave me the materials I needed to perform the task he hired me for. This does <u>not</u> give him the right to steal my credits.

"The Room" was a success! Success in this case is measured in popularity, fan base and magnitude of interest. Yes, it's a bizarre, stupid, absurd little film. It's also a wee bit hypnotic. Ninety-nine minutes of carnage and mayhem that compels you to watch; and then sears your eyeballs with images you'll never forget. Yes, it's an auto wreck. BUT, it's a highly successful auto wreck. I Directed this auto wreck and I did it on purpose. That's the truth and I stand by it. Did I make this a successful film all by myself? No, of course not! Tommy Wiseau would have you think he created this entire movie by himself. Sorry, that's simply not possible. Nobody makes a movie by themselves.

A movie achieves success because of many factors. Film is a collaborative medium. You have to collaborate at all levels to make an interesting film. And, as ridiculous as it sounds, even "The Room" required a collaborative effort. Without the insane pages Tommy wrote and his bizarre allure on film, there would be no movie. I needed the crazy words; and, I most definitely needed his crazy face. I succeeded in achieving my goals. I Directed Tommy Wiseau on film and shared him with the world. That was the point. That was the fun! I Directed the man and his words. He resisted... I compelled and argued... directing, to a large extent, involves manipulating and pushing your actors to do things your way.

Tommy was on set as my lead actor. This was the ONLY reason he was ever on set. He was there to act. Period. No exceptions. He was there to act... and he was miles outside of his comfort zone. Priceless, right? Every scene in the film that featured Johnny would begin with Tommy asking me, "Sandy, how do you want me to do this?" This is what all actors ask their Directors! Mr. Director, how do you want me to do this scene? This process between Directors and actors has been in place for nearly 100 years. This process on "The Room" was more psychological fun than a barrel of psychotic monkeys! Any other interpretation of this film is a waste of time and a pure fabrication.

For fourteen years, I have listened to Tommy smear my reputation and my character. I always figured eventually, "The Room" and Tommy Wiseau would fade away into obscurity. To my utter amazement, it's starting to feel like this film is never going to fade away. I feel just like Al Pacino when he said, "They keep pulling me back in!" He said that in "Godfather 3," a movie just as dumb as "The Room." Sorry, Sophia...

The Franco/Rogen movie, "The Disaster Artist," will be released and distributed world-wide. Seth Rogen is playing me – which is fairly surreal to say the least. I have never been consulted by anybody involved with this production as to the truth about "The Room" and my role in its creation. Seth has never bothered to actually talk to me. I suspect accuracy will be traded for laughs, and the truth will be a bloody casualty on Day 1 of shooting. This film will have an impact on my life and career, whether I want it to or not. To date, neither Seth, James nor anybody else attached to the production of "The Disaster Artist" has bothered to discuss the character and dialogue of

Sandy Schklair prior to, or during, this entire production.

As I stated previously, the producers of this project called me once – once! The day after I gave a fifteen minute phone interview to The Daily Mail and used the word "snubbed." They called to "open lines of communication so I wouldn't feel snubbed." I guess they read the article. Nothing was discussed other than their repetition of the phrase, "We wanted to open lines of communication." Okay... The lines of communication are open... Now what?! Say something! Say anything! This phone conversation was as superficial as a phone conversation can possibly be. Absolutely nothing substantive was discussed or mentioned. How will I be portrayed? How will I appear on film? What lies will be told about me in the interest of raising box office revenues? These are fair questions, are they not? If Seth Rogen were playing you, wouldn't you want these questions answered?

The documentary, "Room Full of Spoons" is also being released this year by its Director, Rick Harper. I know this film will tell the truth; but, who will listen? Tommy Wiseau is using every nasty, dirty trick at his disposal to get this film blacklisted so nobody will see it. He told Rick he will pull "The Room" from any art house that shows "Room Full of Spoons." This documentary tells the truth and Tommy Wiseau is obviously terrified of the truth. Were I standing in Tommy's shoes, I would be terrified as well. His questionable ethics are about to revealed to the world. This also explains why the frequency of his idiotic video uploads to YouTube is increasing.

The book, "The Disaster Artist," written by Greg Sestero and Tom Bissell, was written with neither Greg nor Tom consulting me. They told their version of the story and, once again, my involvement was downplayed and skewed. Once again, the truth was ignored in the interest of perpetuating the fairy tale that Tommy Wiseau Directed this film. Greg is a nice guy and I feel empathy for him. Unfortunately, Greg was stuck between the proverbial rock and the Tommy.

Yes, I am the man who Directed "The Room." I have watched everybody surrounding this film profit from my work. I have <u>never</u> asked for more money, regardless of what you may hear or read on the internet. I say to <u>anyone</u> who wants to point a finger at me and make accusations, PROVE IT! Or, keep your damn opinions to yourself.

Here's a better idea. You think maybe I'm full of shit? You think maybe I've lied? You want to judge me? Fine. Put in your time. Try surviving a Hollywood film career for 25 years. Then, you can judge me. Any film professional who reads this book will recognize the truth immediately.

Movies... books... documentaries... articles... podcasts... all for this absurd, ridiculous, over-the-top, craziness called, "The Room?!" I'm shocked! I'm stunned! I'm amazed and mystified! I'm absolutely delighted! I would say my stupid little movie got noticed, wouldn't you? I always took the high road and avoided the chaos surrounding this movie. It's now 2017 and fourteen years have passed. The movie has turned into a runaway freight train... and I'm tied to the tracks. I've now adopted the same philosophy I used when I made the movie. I'm going to try and steer the train wreck into a safe place and make sure nobody gets hurt.

I have been left with absolutely no choice whatsoever but to write this book.

And so… I have.

YES, I DIRECTED "THE ROOM"

The TRUTH about directing the "Citizen Kane of Bad Movies"

by

Sandy Schklair